WORKBOOK

PARENTING THE CHILD *you have*

Implement Human Design into Your Family and Life

AYPRIL PORTER

Parenting the Child You Have Workbook
Implement Human Design into Your Family and Life

In this world of digital information and rapidly-changing technology, some citations do not provide exact page numbers or credit the original source. We regret any errors, which are a result of the ease with which we consume information.

Disclaimer: This workbook is for informational and educational purposes only. The information and education provided is not intended or implied to supplement or replace professional medical treatment, advice, and/or diagnosis.

Cover Artwork Design by: Imogen Porter and Jeff Porter

An Imprint for GracePoint Publishing (www.GracePointPublishing.com)

GracePoint Matrix, LLC
624 S. Cascade Ave, Suite 201
Colorado Springs, CO 80903
www.GracePointMatrix.com
Email: Admin@GracePointMatrix.com

SAN # 991-6032

A Library of Congress Control Number has been requested and is pending.

ISBN: (Paperback) 978-1-961347-13-7
eISBN: 978-1-961347-14-4

Books may be purchased for educational, business, or sales promotional use.
For bulk order requests and price schedule contact:
Orders@GracePointPublishing.com

TABLE OF CONTENTS

WELCOME

Hi and welcome to *Parenting the Child You Have Workbook: Implement Human Design into Your Family and Life.* This workbook was designed to accompany my bestselling book *Parenting the Child You Have: Re-Imagining the Parent-Child Relationship Through the Lens of Human Design.* I'm Aypril Porter, your guide for this journey. I am a 5/2 Emotional Authority Projector on the left angle Cross of Masks 2. I have shared a link (through the QR code in the back of the book) for you to view my chart if you're interested because what I share here is based on my view of the world and my experiences. This is important because I want you to know that anything I say here should be run through your internal filter for you and your life while keeping in mind who I am as author of this content. Likely you were drawn to me because you have similar or complementary aspects in your chart. However, this doesn't mean that our charts will look alike. In Human Design, this is referred to as being on the same fractal.

Before we go any further, I would like to be clear that you do not have to be a parent to benefit from this content and experience. You may be a parent, a foster parent, a stepparent, an auntie or uncle, a caregiver, or anything in between. You may not be a parent at all but have a curiosity about exploring your own childhood and how it shaped you into the person you are today. Or you may be an adult child who is caring for aging or ill parents and is realizing that all of those old patterns you thought you'd left in childhood when you moved out of the house have come crashing back into your life, and now it has become necessary to explore them and find a new way forward for peace in your life. I invite you into this process to explore your lived experience with deep curiosity, open to challenging what you believe to be the truth, and to seeing it through new eyes. I have found that deep relief, freedom, forgiveness, and compassion can be found by looking at our charts and our family's charts through the lens of Human Design. Whether or not your family or caregivers are still on this earthly plane, if you have their birth information to see their unique Human Design, your mind will be expanded by viewing them and yourself through this lens. I also offer readings for deceased family members if you'd like support in exploring this area.

I want this to feel like a journey that you can dip your toes into when you feel like it, rather than a to-do list of a workbook you have to get through, sitting on your shelf taunting you that you need to complete it. Think of it more as a journal prompt book you can use repeatedly and with any preferred paper, writing tool, computer, or device you choose.

I hope that you find the prompts and information to be useful. You will find that this information is laid out in a manner similar to my book *Parenting the Child You Have.* And, like the book, I suggest you start at the beginning and work your way through, then come back and dig into any areas you want to re-explore as you journey through.

You'll want something to write on and something to write with, and if you're anything like me, you'll want to grab something that feels luxurious to write upon and a pen that feels smooth and joyful to write with. Choose a color that brings you joy, delight, and curiosity or connects you to your child self. Do you remember those pens with twelve or more colors in one pen, and you could switch back and forth with just a click? I love those. Maybe you do too? Of course, you can also write on your computer, however, if possible, I recommend real pen and paper so you can connect more intimately with your thoughts. Alternatively, if you have a hard time finding the time to sit and write or if writing is a challenge for you, or if you tend to overthink things when you try to write them down, I invite you to use your voice memos on your phone to respond to the prompts. Using voice memos offers a different level of insight when you listen to your breath, tone, and emotion in your voice. Choose what works for you, or experiment if you're not sure, and see what feels good.

HOW TO USE THIS WORKBOOK

This workbook is meant to be digested over time. It is not something that you will sit with, take in, and work through in one or two sittings. It takes time to work with these aspects of your childhood, parenting, and day-to-day life, while reflecting, investigating, and integrating what you're realizing and learning about yourself.

This process is not about judgment or criticism of yourself, your parents, or your parenting. We do the best we can with what we have, and when we know better, we have the opportunity to do better. It's not helpful to go back and blame ourselves or our parents for what we, or they, didn't know. My hope is that you will find peace and acceptance through this process.

Acceptance doesn't mean approval or resignation, but it can be an empowered choice to see what is or was and be willing to accept it and choose how you wish to move forward in a way that tells a more empowering story, for yourself and your children. This process is meant to be explored through the lens of possibility and with a healthy dose of curiosity.

If you feel triggered by any of the prompts in this book, please seek professional help if needed. There can be long-standing, deep familial and ancestral wounds that come up in regard to parenting, and with the right support, you can free yourself and future generations from having to repeat these patterns. While there can be a great deal learned from this self-exploration, sometimes it's bigger than we can process on our own. Take care of yourself and ask for the support you need.

I suggest moving through no more than one section every week to allow yourself time to integrate. And if it takes much longer, that is perfect too. There is no rush to get to your best life, as there is no finish line that we are reaching to mark achievement. We are all in a process, and when we can learn to embrace and be present in the process, we live a full and embodied life with all its ups and downs and twists and turns, and we navigate it with grace.

Special Note About the Journal Prompt Questions

In each section, you will find journal questions that may be answered for yourself—the parent—or your child as you think about how their design affects your relationship with them or how your parent's design affects their relationship with you. I encourage you to go through this workbook multiple times with different relationships in mind and see what you uncover about the parent-child relationships in your life.

INTRODUCTION

We all have parts of ourselves that we hide away. Maybe we hide them away because we've been told by our family that "we don't behave that way" or because we've been bullied by our peers for being different. Or, perhaps we grew up supported and felt like we were unique and special, and when we reached adulthood, the world told us that we needed to fit into its predesigned box so that we could get a good job, buy a house, get married, retire, and on and on. We are all conditioned in both positive and negative ways throughout our lives. The goal is not to escape conditioning but to know yourself well enough and be resilient enough to know what is *you* versus what is *the other*—to be influenced by life, people, and circumstances but not lose your identity trying to be something or someone you're not or hiding away yourself. It's painful when we deny aspects of ourselves because it's "not the norm" or makes others uncomfortable. You can learn to embrace your authentic self, using your Human Design chart as a guide and lessen that pain. Perhaps they're out there somewhere, but I have yet to meet an adult who hasn't dealt with some kind of pain around showing the world who they are as a unique individual. We all experience this conditioning, and we all have an opportunity to shift how we see ourselves and how we show up in the world.

If you've read my book *Parenting the Child You Have: Re-Imagining the Parent-Child Relationship Through the Lens of Human Design* (and I'm assuming you have if you've picked up this workbook), then you know that I am passionate about raising our children to remain connected to their true authentic selves. I believe that your being uniquely you is the greatest gift you give to the world in this life. Your giving yourself permission to be you allows others permission to be themselves too. If you're struggling with allowing yourself to show up for yourself in this way, consider what you would tell your child or friend who was living a life that felt inauthentic and wanted to change. How can you receive the advice that you would give others for yourself?

In this workbook, we will explore the stories that you, as the parent, carry from your own childhood and what you consciously or unconsciously are repeating and expecting from your child(ren). This workbook will ask you to show up and answer as honestly as you can, without judgment, so that you can assess where you're starting from and where you want to go with your role as a parent or adult child. This work *must* come first before we can dive into changing our children's behavior. If you've been a parent for a minute, you know that kids will call you on your bullshit and tell you when you're not doing what you said. When this happens, we can see it as a threat to our authority, or we can view it as an opportunity to look at why we are expecting one thing from our children while holding different expectations for ourselves and how we think that that will help them remain true to themselves as they grow. Our children look to us to lead them, to guide them, and to help them know when they're going off course, but it is *not* our job to "correct" their uniqueness or differences out of them. When we feel secure in ourselves and our own uniqueness, we allow space for and appreciate the differences in others.

Human Design allows us a window into the parts of ourselves that we've tried to deny or hide, and it also shows us what comes naturally to us. It allows us to see not only where we might have challenges along our life's path but where we will find ease and blessings. When we align with our design, we recognize where the world begins and ends around us. By that, I mean we are able to discern who we uniquely are and can honor and give ourselves what we need to thrive while allowing the rest of the world the space and freedom to do the same. As we sink deeper into our authentic selves, we stop trying to control others' behavior, expressions, and interests. We recognize that we don't have to be the same or have the same ideas or behaviors, but we can respect one another and allow each other the space to be uniquely who we are. And as we allow each other to be our authentic selves, we begin to let go of the patterns we've been repeating, often since childhood, of people-pleasing, self-sabotaging, playing small, hiding out, and limiting our own joy for the sake of others.

Let's get started!

CHAPTER ONE

THE HUMAN DESIGN CHART AND TERMINOLOGY

Let's do a quick review of basic terminology in Human Design for anyone who is not very familiar with the language yet and perhaps a refresher for those who have stepped away from it for a while.

Grab a printout of your chart and take some notes on yours if you're still learning the Human Design terminology.

BODYGRAPH CHART

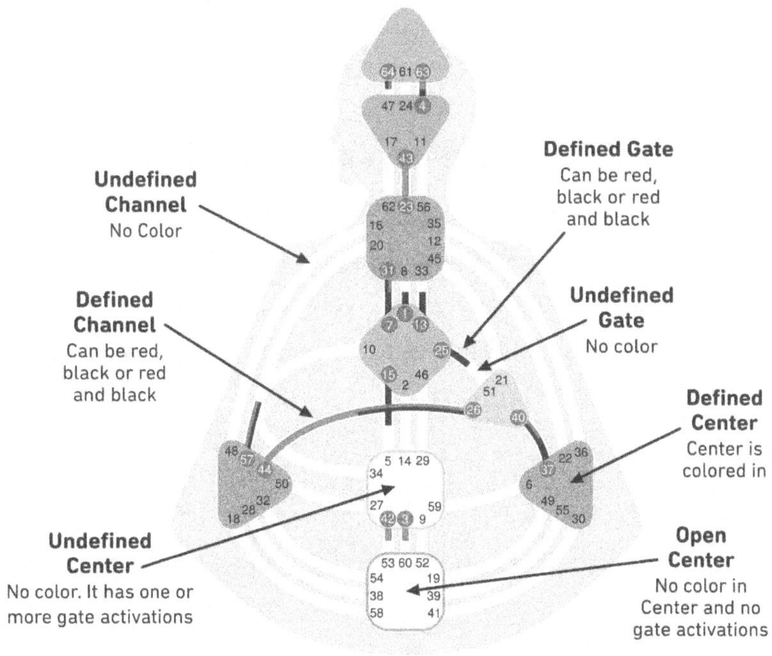

Defined

The definition in the chart is determined at birth and remains consistent throughout our lives. We can think of this as the nature aspect of who we are. Our definition tells us what consistent energy we carry with us wherever we go and what we broadcast to the people around us. This defined energy is not fixed in that it can only be expressed one way and is limiting, but rather that there is a consistency in it we can rely on throughout our lives. This is where we're learning about the energies in the chart through our personal experiences.

Undefined/Open

The areas that are open or undefined in our chart are the areas where we are receiving information and learning about the world, other people, and that energy in our lives. These are areas where we receive the most conditioning, and they correlate with the nurture aspect of who we become. This is where we're learning about the energies in the chart through our relationship experiences.

Conditioned/Not-Self

The conditioned or not-self in Human Design refers to how we live out the expression of our chart that goes against our design. We are conditioned most by the people in our lives. For example, a Projector's Strategy is to wait for the invitation; however, if they live in a conditioned or not-self way, they are impulsive and take action without waiting for recognition and an invitation. Another example would be someone with an open Sacral Center who is continually pushing and working, not knowing when enough is enough, and is living through conditioning to do more physical work than they are designed for which often leads to burn out.

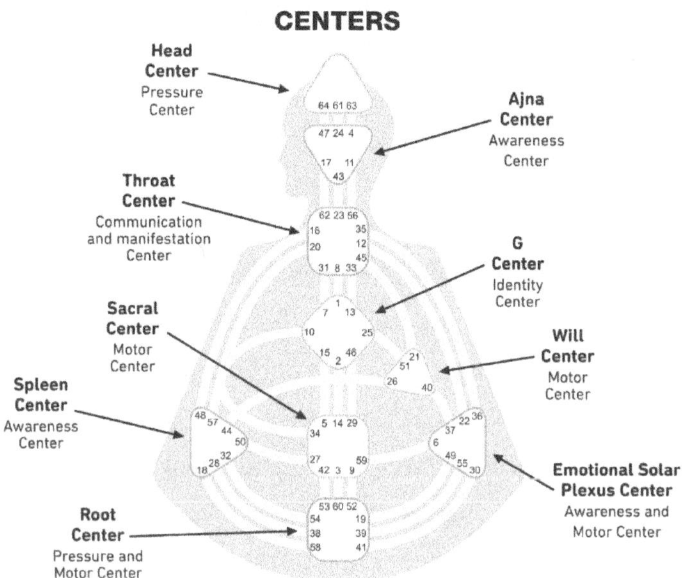

Centers

The chart contains nine energy centers. The chart originally had seven centers, like the chakra system, but in 1781 it underwent a change. Two of the centers split into two each, resulting in the nine-centered beings currently reflected in the charts. The energy centers carry a specific theme and tell us more about the nine main themes of energy in the chart. What is defined is consistent within your centers, and what is open fluctuates depending on who you're around and the environment. These centers are what you will hear most often talked about in Human Design in terms of definition. Clients who have studied their charts before often come to me for a session and tell me that they or their family members *only* have two centers or one channel defined, for example. This is not a game of who has the most defined centers or channels. We all have and experience all of the components in the chart, and the definition shows what is more consistent for us.

Conscious (Black)

The right side of the chart has a list of planetary symbols with the gates and lines listed in black. These represent what gates were activated by the planets in the chart at the moment of birth. The gates listed here are what we can most easily see in ourselves. This side of the chart represents the mind and is labeled as *mind, soul, personality*, or *conscious*, depending on the software used to calculate the chart. Color may vary from black based on the software used, however traditionally this side of the chart is represented in black.

Unconscious (Red)

On the left side of the chart is a duplicate of the list of planetary symbols with the gates and lines listed in red. These represent what gates were activated by the planets in the chart approximately three months before birth. This side of the chart can feel a little more elusive, especially when just learning the energies of the centers, gates, and channels, and is commonly referred to as the unconscious side. This part of the chart represents the physical form (body) and can also be labeled *body, design, life,* or *unconscious,* depending on the software used to calculate the chart. The energy represented on this side of the chart is generally more easily seen by the people in your life than by you. As you begin deconditioning and as you live out more of your life, you'll get more familiar with these aspects of yourself. Color may vary from red based on the software used, however traditionally this side of the chart is represented in red.

Magnetic Monopole

The conscious and unconscious sides of the chart are energetically held together through something called the Magnetic Monopole that resides in your G (Identity) Center. You also have a design crystal in the Ajna Center and a personality crystal in the Head Center. These are not actual crystals you could locate, but energetic.

The Magnetic Monopole is like a one-way magnet holding both aspects of your design together, keeping you feeling like one person with different aspects of yourself rather than two completely different people living within the same body. It also aligns us with our life path as it pulls us along our trajectory through space and time.

Gates

The sixty-four gates correlate with the Chinese I Ching hexagrams. While the gates in Human Design represent a separate archetype on their own, we cannot look at them in isolation as we are not merely one of our parts but a synthesis of our entire chart. The gates are located in the centers in the BodyGraph, and their themes correlate to the overarching theme of that energy center. For example, a gate in the G Center will have the theme of love, identity, or direction, while a gate in the Spleen Center will have to do with the immune system, instincts, intuition, timing, or fears. The gates numbered 1-64 are located in the centers and are also connected to the theme of the planet that was highlighting the gate at the moment of birth.

Lines

Each of the sixty-four gates has six possible line activations, creating 384 possible gate activations within a chart. Each of the six lines has a unique theme that correlates with the profile lines. For example, if you have Gate 25.1 activated in your chart, it represents Gate 25, with Line 1 as the specific gate expression. Line one is The Investigator in the profile lines, so this line energy brings investigative qualities to the expression of this gate. This gate has the energy of someone drawn to investigate their spirituality and feel secure in it before sharing it with others. Depending on the software you use, you will see the line written as the number after the decimal (25.1) or as what looks like an exponent (25^1).

Channels

The channels, when defined, create a consistent archetypal theme of that particular channel's energy throughout your whole life. Channel definition in a chart creates definition in the energy centers on either end of the channel. The gates located at each side of a channel have a related theme.

If you look at the BodyGraph now, you'll see, for example, that Gate 12 which is coming out of the right lower side of the Throat Center connects on the other end of that channel through Gate 22 in the Emotional Solar Plexus (ESP). By having both Gate 12 and Gate 22 defined, we now have the defined Channel 12-22 and a defined Throat Center and ESP.

This channel definition in your birth chart originates from what gates were activated by the planets in the personality or design side of your chart. Channels can also be temporarily experienced through connections with other people or as the planets transit through the gates during your life. While these connections through people or planets give us a different understanding of what it is like to embody that energy, they are not as consistent and reliable for us as the channels in our birth chart. The definition in our birth chart is always the same. It is an energy that is consistently there and transmits to the world who we are. The expression of that energy is on a spectrum and is experienced in a variety of ways. When you are around people with different definition in their charts, you will create a temporary experience of what it is like to feel the energy of that gate, channel, or center, which can create an unconscious attraction to people who have the gates defined in their chart that you do not, especially if they complete a channel for you, bridge a split in your definition, or move energy to your Throat Center.

Planets

There are twenty-six total planet activations located in both the conscious and unconscious sides of the birth chart, representing what gate activation was present in each planet at the moment of birth (conscious) and approximately three months before birth (unconscious).

What Do These Planets Represent?

The Sun shows our personality, expression, and life force. It is what we are giving to the world through our unique expression. This is the gift we give to the world by just being our authentic selves. Seventy percent of our chart is expressed through our conscious Sun gate and line.

The Earth is what grounds us and what we need to feel stable to express what is in our Sun. Look to these gates to understand what energy you need to be grounded in.

The North Node is the theme of the second half of your life, after your Uranus Opposition, around age forty. It's considered the breathing-out phase of life.

The South Node is the theme we start in and grow through into our midlife around our Uranus Opposition. It's the breathing-in phase of life.

The Moon is what drives you. It's why we do what we do. If you want to know what drives someone to behave and focus on certain things in their life, look to the themes of the moon.

Mercury is about communication. The gate theme here is what we're here to talk about and share.

Venus is what we value in our relationships and can relate to the mother and mother wounds as well.

Mars is where we experience our youthful lessons, and if we don't learn to master it, it can become a disruptive energy in our lives and potentially cause us to feel like giving up.

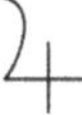

Jupiter is where we receive our blessings and rewards of the lessons Saturn teaches us.

♄

Saturn is what we are here to learn. It is our great teacher when we open to learning the lessons here.

⛢

Uranus is where we are a bit different and is also where we can expect the unexpected. It is our teacher of faith.

♆

Neptune is our spiritual purpose, and it is often veiled, which means that it always feels sort of elusive to us if we go looking for it.

♇

Pluto is where we experience expanse and challenge and where we experience a rebirth. It is often a generational theme as this is a slow-moving planet. You'll see generations of people working through similar themes with the same gates in their Pluto positions in the Human Design charts.

Deconditioning

Deconditioning is the conscious act of coming back to your authentic self. The conditioned/not-self refers to someone living out of their conditioning. This is also referred to as living "off the chart." An example would be if you have an undefined Sacral Center, and you are pushing with your energy all the time without realizing that you are taking in and amplifying the energy around you and that it's not sustainable energy for you; you are living out of your conditioning. You may think that you have all of this energy to "do," but you are not designed to hold that frequency of energy consistently and can tend not to know when enough is enough and burn yourself out.

Conditioning is essentially operating out of the mind and what it thinks we should do. The mind thinks we are designed to operate with our energy based on the conditioning fields we grew up in or live in, rather than honoring the truth that resides in our body's wisdom. As you uncover the truth of who you are and how you're designed, you come back to your authentic self and stop living out of the conditioned self as much.

Kids, on the other hand, have not had the decades of conditioning we have as adults, so they can often drop the conditioning faster than adults. Our job as parents who are awake and aware of Human Design, is to teach our children to honor who they innately are and nourish their authentic selves to remain true to their design.

There is currently a message that is being put out into the self-help/spirituality world that suggests we must decondition from all of the stuff that we have lived through and experienced. And I would remind you that deconditioning is a process, not a destination.

We will always live in a conditioning field. The goal is not to be free from it but to better understand oneself so you can differentiate between what is you, and what you are experiencing through other people and the planetary transits. When you can see the conditioning field for what it is, it can become a learning experience, a place to practice empathy for others and have a greater understanding of humanity.

CHAPTER TWO

WHY UNDERSTANDING YOUR CHILD THROUGH THE LENS OF HUMAN DESIGN IS IMPORTANT

We often have an idea of how we will parent before we ever even come close to actually parenting. We tend to hold deep beliefs about what a good parent does and how a good child behaves. We often have clear pictures of what those roles look like, either based on what our childhood was like or what it was not like.

What so many of us have not really considered until Human Design or some other system came into our lives is how unique our children really are and why that is so wonderful. Yes, we share the same DNA if they are our biological children, but I'm sure you've seen children from the same family that seem completely different despite being raised in the same conditions. Then why are they so different?

Our unique Human Design charts reveal how and why we all are so different. Though there are four main energy types in Human Design, clearly we can see that there are many variations of them, and that is based on the unique energy blueprint we are born into, plus the conditioning we live within.

We have our own personal filters that we see the world through, and if we assume our children will do as we ask or tell and be as we expect them to be, we shut down their ability to express themselves as who they truly are in their hearts.

When we see our children through their unique blueprint, we allow ourselves to see who they are here to be, rather than who we think they should be. We stop generational patterns of control and outdated ways of parenting, and we choose to parent in the way we and our children need. We have the opportunity to stop the continuation of ancestral patterns that were repeated because it's all we knew.

It's not easy as a parent to know if you're doing the right things for your children. I believe that we do the best we can with what we have, and when we know better, we have a responsibility to do better. You now have an amazing tool in your awareness that will help you to look more objectively at your child and their needs and honor what is different about them. They may be vastly different from you, and rather than try to make them more like you or the rest of the family, you can allow them to be themselves with confidence and support.

Imagine if you'd grown up with parents who knew Human Design and would have encouraged you to be your true authentic self. Even if you had really supportive parents, imagine how much more they could have understood and supported you with this information at their fingertips.

Whether you are finding this information before having children, when you have young children, teens, or adult children, it is the perfect time. You can always begin now. It is never too late to try to understand who someone is and support and encourage them to be themselves.

The work you are doing right now will go on generation after generation. Human Design came into the world in 1987, and we are now seeing children that have been raised with this system emerging into the world as adults and raising their children with this tool as well. Only in the last five to ten years have we really seen the traction of this system gaining awareness on a broader scale. Imagine where our kids will be twenty, thirty, or forty years from now. We are changing the paradigm of how we parent as a society by simply focusing on our own parenting strategies. When we see our stories as they show up in our children, we have an opportunity to see ourselves in a new light and give ourselves what we may not have gotten as children.

Though I believe that most of our parents do the best they can with what they have, the ones who haven't done so great or who have done so terribly, I wonder not so much what is wrong with them but rather what happened to them. What were their childhoods like? Who didn't see them for the amazing person they are capable of being? Who broke their spirit? When did their child self get the message that they couldn't do better? And whether or not you're able to right now, I send love to them all, as well as you. As Dr. Martin Luther King, Jr. famously said, "Hate cannot drive out hate; only love can do that." Wherever you are on your journey with your relationship with your parents, I support you. I don't expect you to give that kind of love when living in a place of hurt or fear. I'm not glossing over your lived experience or telling you to forget about it. Absolutely not. I only want the best for you. And I understand that we build walls around ourselves to protect ourselves, and only when we feel strong enough and safe enough can we begin to take those walls down. I would never push you to take them down before you're ready. Know that no matter what has happened to you in this lifetime, no matter what you've experienced, you are loved. Love is universal. It is given to you for simply existing. You are the Divine, and the Divine is you, and you are loved.

Human Design allows us to see our parents through a unique lens, too, especially as adults. We carry these childlike understandings of who our parents are from our childhood formed by our child brains who thought they knew and understood the whole picture. I would invite you to consider how you might see your parents as just people trying to do what they thought was right without a map to guide them.

My experience with Human Design has been one of deep freedom by allowing myself to see the people in my life and family who have challenged me the most through a new lens and hold more compassion for them, which I didn't expect.

I wonder what *you'll* find on this journey...

How We Do the Work

Using my five-step process outlined here, you will decondition from the limiting beliefs holding you back from living life and parenting in the way you want. I encourage you to use these five steps as you journey through the workbook and find elements of your chart that feel out of alignment with how you show up in the world to uncover more of the truth of who you are. This process will help you let go of patterns you inherited that you no longer need and are ready to be free from.

1. Seeing What Is

You'll need to allow yourself to pull back enough to see the big picture and what is actually happening rather than only what you perceive is happening. To do this, I invite you to sit down with a pen and paper or something to type on if you prefer and think about an instance where there was conflict or misunderstanding between you and your child or within the family from your current perspective and thought process. Spend some time writing about any thoughts, feelings, and behaviors you notice. Make sure to note any judgments you have and let them be there. What do you think *should* have happened? How *should* you or anyone else in this picture have behaved?

Next, you'll write about the same situation as if you were sitting outside of your house or environment where the event occurred and pretend it was another family that you were looking in on. To be able to take on this more objective view, you'll need to look at this situation as if you were a stranger looking in on your family. If it helps, create a persona that you could adopt as you view your family and self through this new lens. Write about the event as if you were watching the neighbors or someone you don't know. How would you describe each character? How would you describe the events taking place? How would you feel if you were watching this interaction in someone else's family? What criticisms or judgments would you have? Would you have more compassion for any of the characters? Spend some time again writing what you see. What do you notice in each of the characters? What do you notice about the character who is playing you in this scene? You don't need to do anything to change it yet. All you need to do is be open to observing what actually is.

2. Allowing What Is

Now that you've identified some aspects that you might not have seen or noticed before, how can you allow those aspects to be there without judging them? It can be difficult but try not to criticize your experience or any judgments you may notice. Just allow them to be there through this process and feel what you feel. With this step, we're practicing allowing ourselves to sit with the emotions that come up to allow them to reveal their wisdom and show us what we need to know to move forward rather than pushing them away, thereby packing our emotional bags heavier and heavier. You may notice physical discomfort as you sit with the emotions and meet them. You don't have to meet them head-on right away. Crack the door open so you can get a sense of what is there, and as you feel more confident, you'll become more comfortable sitting with them longer. This will become easier over time as rather than just looking at an emotion that feels scary or overwhelming and not knowing what to do with it, you're going to use this five-step process and your Human Design chart to take action that is empowering.

If, for example, remembering an argument with your teenager, you see yourself not listening and instead criticizing your child, how can you allow that observation to be there without judging it, hiding it, or wanting it to be different? We're going to work to shift this, but for now, we just need to look at the truth of how it happened in your mind, what you felt and experienced, as well as any secondary emotions that might arise, such as shame, embarrassment, frustration, or anger.

3. Releasing the Pain, Judgment, and Past

One of my favorite tools is the emotional freedom technique (EFT or tapping) to tap on the things that come up when you begin to see what is and allow what is. If you're new to tapping, scan the QR code in the back of the book to view a video of me walking you through a simple tapping sequence.

If you're familiar with tapping, here are a couple of setup phrases you can use to get started if they feel true to you.

- Even though I judge myself for (behaving/feeling/reacting this way), I deeply and completely love and accept myself.
- Even though I wish I could go back in time and change this, I deeply and completely love and accept myself.
- Even though I feel (ashamed/angry/unheard/unloved/unvalued, etc.), I deeply and completely love and accept myself.

If you're new to tapping, you may notice that these seem like very negative self-talk statements; however, tapping works by meeting the current truth where it is, acknowledging it, and letting yourself know that you're still lovable, you still accept yourself, and there is nothing bad or wrong about you for feeling those things.

You don't have to stay stuck in this negative-sounding space, and as you tap with these sequences (make them custom to you and your situation), you'll shift how you feel about your experiences. These internal shifts change your reaction to your family and allow you to open enough to allow healing into this space and begin to shift the patterns that are not serving you anymore.

Other ways to release the stories of the past that you've been holding onto are as follows:

Journaling—this can be done in any way that feels good to you. Write a letter to someone, write and draw, bullet journal, or speak your thoughts into a recording device.

Wild-mind writing is a style which comes from the work of Natalie Goldberg. The basic premise is that you set a timer for five or ten minutes, sit down with a pen and paper, and just start writing. You don't worry about filtering, editing, grammar, or structure, just write whatever comes to your mind. At first, you might feel your mind is blank. Write that. "My mind is blank, and I can't think of anything to write." As you sit, keep your pen moving. Doodle. Do whatever it takes to keep that pen moving, and as you do, your subconscious will begin to bring things to the page that want to be heard. When you're done, scan over your pages and see what themes you notice. What words stand out? What words do you want to erase and hide from? Those are the important things. They are what need your attention.

A coaching session with a life coach or Human Design life coach, where your coach can help you to see and release your stories that are no longer serving you may be helpful.

Create art and allow your mind to show you what you're needing to express or give attention to.

Garden or connect with the earth. Let your mind carry you where it needs to go while you touch nature, and let her wisdom guide you.

Connect with nature as you did as a child. Make mud pies and headbands of flowers. Build forts and climb trees. Write your name in the sand at the beach, swim in a lake, make snow angels, plant flowers, grow vegetables, swing at the park, go roller skating, bike riding, for a run, or just sit in the sunshine unplugged and feel the warmth upon your skin. Skip rocks, go fishing, or run through the sprinkler. Do what feels good as you connect back to the core of who you are and remember what was once important to you.

Practice gratitude. What are three things that you are grateful for each day? Write them down.

Ask your child self what he/she/they didn't get or what he/she/they needed to hear when that memory was formed. What would your adult self tell that child now? What does your child self need to hear from your adult self?

Find a trusted person to be your sounding board and talk about what you're feeling or thinking.

4. Getting Curious About What Is Possible

Now that you've observed what may be happening in your family or relationships, you'll spend some time considering what other outcomes are possible. This is where you begin to dream and create more of what you want. How could you show up in your life differently? Before you let your mind take over and start telling you all the reasons why it can't be different or defending why it is the way it is, allow yourself to dream a little... or a lot! What would your most desired outcome be? And if that's too much to consider, what is one step better than where you are now?

It could also be that you feel like things are handled just right or are the best they can be given your circumstance. If that's where you are, how can you accept it? Acceptance does not mean approval. You can accept things as they are and still strive to make them different. This is where you can find the motivation to make the changes you want in your relationships.

As you go through this contemplative work, consider revisiting the instance or situation you wrote about in step one and see if you still feel the same about it now. Often as we learn more, we can revisit old patterns and situations and see them differently and then become more open to changes that we weren't before. As we heal these patterns and the beliefs we've carried for so long by simply seeing ourselves and each other through another lens, we begin to see a different picture than before.

5. Taking Aligned Action

Once you know how you want to do things differently, it's just a matter of putting it into action. Action is imperfect. We can't expect that we will do things the way we'd like to 100 percent of the time. We are humans, after all, with histories and wounds that come up again and again as we peel back the layers of conditioning and hurt we have experienced to reveal a deeper awareness of our truths. It's all about practice. Practice over perfection. Just show up and try. You don't have to always get it right. Be willing to say you are sorry and try again. Commit to imperfect action.

As you move through this workbook, use this five-step process to challenge any limiting beliefs that you carry and move through them. For some patterns it may take several iterations of these steps to create meaningful change. Repeating this process for one story or belief you carry is not failing, it's simply allowing you to peel back more layers and shows your commitment to the work. Some stories are just really ingrained and there are many facets to look at to truly liberate ourselves from them. Keep loving on yourself and working with them and remember that these patterns you're shifting are both for you and future generations.

Getting Connected to Our Inner Child

Before we dive into the specific areas of your Human Design chart, or that of your child or parent, we're going to take some time to consider where you are starting from and what you'd like to get out of this work by connecting to your inner child.

With the subject of parenting, we must consider our own childhood experiences in addition to our current parenting experiences. If you don't feel like you're in a good place to explore childhood memories, skip this exercise or come back to it when you are ready or have received any professional support you need.

We're going to spend some time journaling about your childhood experience. First, if you have a picture of yourself at about the age of five, please have it in front of you while we go through this exercise. If you do not have a photograph of yourself in childhood, spend a few minutes and visualize yourself around the age of about five in a good memory.

You may listen to the audio recording to walk you through this exercise if you choose, which can be found through the QR code in the back of this book.

Find a quiet place that feels comfortable. You may sit in a chair with your feet on the floor, or perhaps you feel more comfortable sitting cross-legged on the floor. Or lie down in the grass and stare up at the sky. While looking at your picture, take a deep breath through your nose, pulling the air down all the way into your belly. Breathe in so deeply that you see your belly rise with your inhalation, and then slowly exhale your breath through your mouth. Take another deep breath in, and as you exhale, let your mind slow down and focus on your picture, or imagine you're looking at an old family video of when you were a child. If you feel difficult things arise, keep breathing and know that I support you in taking care of you. If you need to stop this exercise, please do. If you feel okay, let's continue.

When you were five, what were you doing that brought you joy? Were you creative? Athletic? Social? A bookworm?

Where did you love spending your time? Did you have a favorite place? Perhaps a place in nature, a room in your house, a fort in the woods, or a treehouse. Or maybe it was a friend's house or school.

What was your favorite thing to do? Did you like to draw, read, play an instrument, play sports, adventure, or explore?

Who were your friends? What were they like? Are you still friends, or did they drift out of your life?

What did you have in common with those friends?

How did you feel different from your friends or family? Did you like different activities? Play different sports? Prefer adventures to staying at home, or maybe you were a homebody?

How were you like your friends or family? What did you have in common?

Think of an instance when you let go and just lived in the moment. Try and hold onto that feeling of freedom of living in the moment when you were having fun and felt free to be yourself without anyone telling you what you were capable of, and the world felt full of possibilities.

Try to hold onto this energy of being your younger child self and grab your journal, notebook, or computer if you prefer, and answer the following questions. Feel free to give yourself space to contemplate them one at a time or come back to them several times to complete.

Questions and Journal Prompts

1. What does it mean to you to be different from everyone else now as an adult?
2. What did it mean for you to feel different from others when you were a child?
3. What beliefs do you have about being different or the same as others?
4. What beliefs do you now hold that you know are not helpful to you?
    a. How do you know they aren't helpful?
    b. What determines what is a helpful belief versus what is a harmful belief to you?
5. What emotion or feeling does it evoke in you to think of yourself as the same or different from others?
6. Let's take that emotion or feeling a step further here and describe where you feel that feeling in your body.
    a. Can you describe any sensations it has? Does it have any words, colors, sounds, or voices?
7. When you think about your childhood, what feelings or words come to mind?
    a. What feelings does that bring up in you?
    b. Is there a specific childhood memory that surfaces?
8. How old is your child now?
    a. What were you experiencing as a child of that age?
9. What limiting beliefs do you hold about children in general? I.e., "children should be seen and not heard," "children should be well-behaved," "children should be catered to," "children should get everything a parent can give them," "children should be respectful of their elders," etc.
10. What expansive beliefs do you hold about children in general? I.e., "children are our future, and we should support them," "children are capable beings," "children need adventure, explorations, and time to create," etc.

11. What beliefs and values do you hold as important for your children?
12. What is one thing you and your child bump up against regularly in your relationship?
13. What does it mean for your child to be different from everyone else?
    a. What beliefs do you have about how they will experience life based on their differences?
14. What roles do you define as more masculine or feminine?
    a. In your mind, is it okay for people to express themselves or be drawn to tasks, careers, styles, etc., that are more historically associated with a specific gender?
15. Where do your beliefs come from?
    a. Were you raised with parents who told you what to believe?
    b. Were you allowed to daydream and get curious about life, people, religions, cultures, etc.?
    c. Were you raised in a religious faith that had strict rules on behavior, sexuality, gender roles, dress, careers, etc.?
    d. How has that impacted you?
16. What values do you hold in your life?
    a. Are there any values that you inherited from your family, culture, or environment that no longer feel aligned with you?
    b. If yes, how can you release those values as your own while still respecting those values in your family, community, and environment?

It can be helpful after doing this exercise to either spend some time alone to contemplate what you just explored or connect with others and process the thoughts that came up for you.

CHAPTER THREE

ENERGY TYPE AND STRATEGY

Before we get started with the details, grab your and anyone in your family's charts that you want to work with. I prefer to print them, as I'm a visual learner, and it's easier for me when referencing several charts to lay them out side by side; however, a digital copy will work great too. If you need a chart, go to www.geneticmatrix.com or to your preferred chart software now and run your charts.

You'll need the exact birth date, time, and location of everyone you want to run a chart for.

If you are running charts for parents or people who you have no access to their birth time, you will want to run their chart every couple of hours throughout the day to see if their Type or Authority changes. Then, if you can get a sense of which one seems to fit more (assuming they weren't living a heavily conditioned life the entire time you knew them), you should be able to get a sense of their chart. **However, it will not be totally accurate without the exact information, so take it in as possible information. If the birth time is inaccurate, it will be a guesstimate at best.** We tend to use 12:01 pm local time if we don't have a time or estimate but know that it will not be as accurate as if you have an actual birth time. If you notice Type, Authority, or Profile changes throughout the day, keep these aspects in mind as you explore their chart.

You'll want to look at all the charts and make a list of who has what energy type. Highlight, or make note of which of the energy type characteristics you notice in each person, such as the energy type's purpose, Strategy, not self, and aligned self-emotional themes. Write in any other notable characteristics about each person.

Who are all of the Manifestors in the family?

Who are all of the Generators in the family?

Who are all of the Manifesting Generators in the family?

Who are all of the Projectors in the family?

Who are all of the Reflectors in the family?

We'll explore these in more depth in the coming pages; however, here are a few characteristics of each energy type as an overview.

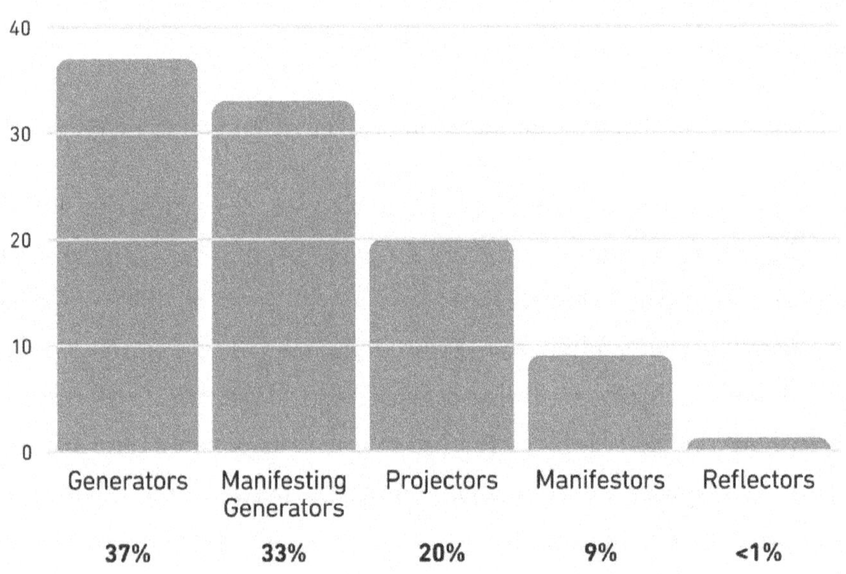

Manifestors -

- No Sacral definition.
- Emotional signatures of anger or peace.
- Initiating energy.
- Restless energy at times if feeling suppressed from taking action on something they want to do.

- Need cycles of rest.
- May sneak around to do what they want because they feel they will be stopped if they tell you first.

Generators -

- Sacral definition.
- Emotional signatures of frustration or satisfaction.
- Can have high energy, bouncing with energy in the evening if they haven't had enough physical exertion.
- Can burn out and keep getting up and going to work.
- Can tend to people-pleasing through their conditioning.
- Will do the work that no one else wants to do and then get frustrated by it.

Manifesting Generators -

- Sacral definition.
- Emotional signatures of frustration and anger, or satisfaction.
- Has a lot of energy, always doing multiple things at once, and *seem* like they can't stick with things.
- Jumps around to several professions/sports/activities and if told just to pick something and stick with it, can lead to frustration and anger.
- Quits before they reach achievement out of frustration if they don't understand their own process of how they work.
- Multi-passionate.
- Learns where to take shortcuts but often has to repeat steps as they learn.

Projectors -

- No Sacral definition.
- Emotional signatures of bitterness or success.

- Organize people/things and can tend to be bossy when they are younger if the people around them don't understand their needs, and as adults if they don't learn how to wait for the invitation and value themselves.
- Great at seeing the big picture and how to improve efficiency with energy.
- Observes people and their behaviors.
- They are here to guide but must be invited.
- Interact best with one person at a time.

Reflectors -

- No Sacral definition.
- Emotional signatures of disappointment or surprise/delight.
- Adapt to whoever they're around: They can blend into their surroundings, or really stand out.
- Need alone time.
- Takes a long time to make a decision and pressuring them makes things more difficult.
- The barometer of their world, they show us where we are not living in alignment.

You may notice that your family consists primarily of one or two energy types. This is very normal. Our designs actually come from our grandparents, so you'll see similarities in your chart to your grandparents, though this does not mean that the energy type will be the same. You'll see themes repeated in the charts every other generation, which means you'll notice similarities in your child's chart to your parent's charts. This is no accident. I mentioned in *Parenting the Child You Have* that our children are here to teach us, and Human Design shows us where those lessons are.

Consider for a moment that the conditioning field you grew up in with your family made you who you are, and then you went out into the world and learned how to be your own person and grew your own family.

Now, as you are raising your family, you have the energies that your parents carried through their unique energy blueprint brought back into your home for you to experience again through your children.

At times it can be incredibly frustrating, but it can also allow for a great deal of growth when you do the work to nourish yourself back to the truth of who you are, authentically and unapologetically.

The same energies you experienced and that provoked you as a child will show up in your children and evoke a response in the areas where you still need to grow and develop. Some of these are from our lifetimes, and some are from generations past. It is important to acknowledge that most of the time, our parents don't do things to harm us intentionally. Still, they too are children who inherited ancestral wounds that need (or needed) tending, and they may not have had the tools available to help them heal. We continue to pass these lessons and wounds down through the generations until we choose to do the work of healing ourselves. The healing we do not only helps us to live a more deeply aligned life but also releases future generations from the pain of these wounds.

As an example, let's look at this parent-child ancestral pattern further.

Consider for example, if you have an open Will Center and your father and your daughter both have defined Will Centers. Growing up, if your father exerted his willpower over you with his ideals of who and how you should be, it may have limited your expression of your authentic self around your family.

You then went out into the world and created friendships and partnerships that allowed you to express those parts of yourself that you didn't get to while growing up. Everything in life is cruising along just fine until suddenly, you realize that some of those same old feelings of being controlled or told how to be, are coming up when you're engaging with your child.

It's not necessarily over the same things, but that feeling you had that told you it was not okay to be yourself gets triggered through a willful response and your child's ability to outlast you in an argument. You notice feeling defeated, and suddenly you realize that you have old stuff to work through.

Noticing these feelings creates an opportunity to heal those parts of you that were wounded/repressed through the overexertion of a parent's willpower so that you can stand in your own authority and authenticity when engaging with other willful people. And because you're parenting a child with a defined Will Center, you'll get a lot of opportunities to work through this energy dynamic regularly.

As we move through this parent-child exploration process, consider how these themes have played out in your life through your relationship with your parents and now through your children. Also, consider that if you have aging parents, these challenging dynamics may come back again if you become a primary caregiver, or they move in with you and you haven't done the work to heal and decondition these parts of yourself.

You can skip through to the energy types that apply to you, your children, or your parents, depending on what relationships you're working on right now. Each section has prompts for the energy type, whether you are the adult or child of that energy type. Though I do recommend getting familiar with all energy types, as you will encounter people with all the energy types at some point in your life, even if you don't know their charts. If you understand the energy types and you come into contact or relationship with people you don't understand, you can consider if they may be a different energy type than you and allow them to have their processes and ways of being in the world without it having to be similar to yours. Human Design allows us to have more compassion for the people around us and how we are all different, allowing us to embrace our differences.

Remember that we are more than our energy types. Please don't let yourself get caught up in these categories as labels and let them define you or limit you. You, my friend, are limitless.

Manifestors

Non-Sacral Energy Type—Approximately 8-9 Percent of the Population

Purpose: To initiate and bring new ideas into form

Strategy: To wait for their inner creative drive, no matter how irrational it may seem to others, to tell them when it is the right time to take action and then inform those around them who will be affected.

Signature Emotion: Peace

Signature Not-Self Emotion: Anger

As a Manifestor, you are here to initiate the world into new ideas, processes, and ways of being, but you can't do that if you don't feel powerful, creative, peaceful, aligned, and rested. If you aren't feeling those things, let's take a look at where some of that misalignment may be coming from. Complete only the questions you feel aligned with and are called to answer. You may find you want to come back at another time and feel called to answer other questions you initially left blank, and that's okay. This is your journey, and you can choose how you approach it.

A Quick Reminder of What Manifestor Parents Need to Learn

(For more details, reference chapter five in *Parenting the Child You Have,* the book)

1. **Informing**—If you are a Manifestor parent, you need to inform the people around you of what you plan to do so they can adjust to your Manifestor energy being there or not. And also, so you can proceed with your initiating without being interrupted. Once a Manifestor gets stopped in their creation process, they can have difficulty getting started again. If you are frequently interrupted in your processes, are tired, or are not informed of what is going on in your family or around you that may affect you, your signature emotion of anger may show up in your family interactions.

   You also need to inform your family that you need to be informed of things that will affect you. For example, if you expect to have the house to yourself to work on some projects, and then their plans change, and you now don't feel like you'll have that uninterrupted time to follow your inner creative drive, you may see your not-self emotion of anger show up, and it may be directed at your family.

2. **Anger**—The anger simply tells you when your process is interrupted or when you're not allowing yourself to rest; it's not who you are. Please do not confuse

this emotion with your identity. It is a guide to help you know when you are off track and signal that you need to realign and take care of your needs. Lessen your time feeling angry by informing those who will be affected or who may interrupt you of what you need.

3. **Delegating**—Because you don't have the sustainable energy of someone with a defined Sacral Center, you'll need rest cycles. Learning to delegate and share responsibilities will be crucial to get your rest cycles so you can refresh and be ready to initiate your next big thing.
4. **Rest cycles**—You'll need to ensure you are resourced before taking on the next thing. Cycles of rest are critical. You cannot keep going in creation mode non-stop. The rest cycles allow you to recharge so your creativity can be fresh and exciting and give you the energy to birth your next new thing into the world.
5. **Handing things over to others to complete**—Another thing you'll need to learn is that you don't have to be the one to finish everything that you start. It's okay to ask others for help or support. I know this can be hard because society and possibly your parents have told you your entire life that you need to stick with things and follow them to completion. But Manifestors don't have that seemingly endless energy supply that people with defined Sacral Centers have. This is where people-pleasing can sneak up on you, so be mindful that you are listening to your body and taking breaks when you need them. Sometimes that means daily breaks, and other times you may need weeks or months between big creative initiations.
6. **Impact**—Lastly, you'll need to be aware that your energy impacts those around you. Your presence or absence is felt when you enter or leave a room. Without informing, everyone may wonder where you are going and what you will do. Inform them, and they'll learn to give you more space rather than ask you constantly what you're doing or where you're going.
7. **Emotional Authority—**If you have an Emotional Authority, you need to give yourself time to move through your wave and feel into your decisions. For example, if you say yes to your child and you're not rested, you may see your not-self emotion of anger. See Emotional Authority in chapter four, for more details.

Journal Prompts for Manifestor Parents

First, we will explore your *childhood* experience as a Manifestor.

1. What was your curiosity like as a child?
2. Did you have a secret life as a child or teenager, if so write about any feelings you have about it.
3. What did you like to invent or be passionate about as a child? What did it feel like when you were following your creative impulses?
4. How strict were your parents with you?
5. Do you feel like your parents understand you and your needs, or not?
6. How were you allowed to be or punished for wanting to be creative and explore?
7. Were you allowed cycles of rest?
8. Were you praised for your doing? This is often an area where parents with other energy types do not understand the Manifestor's need for downtime and inadvertently teach their Manifestor children to keep going and doing rather than listen to their bodies. Because it feels good to be rewarded with praise, this can lead a Manifestor to try to keep up with all the doing to feel loved, valued, and seen. Consider what your lived experience as a Manifestor child was. What was your relationship to doing and receiving praise as a child?
9. Were you raised in a family of Generators/Manifesting Generators? If so, what was that like looking back through the lens of Human Design as you now know it?

Next, let's explore your *adulthood* experience as a Manifestor.

1. What is your relationship to people-pleasing?
2. When do you feel the most creative or inspired? Are there places where you feel more creative? Are there people or places that make it difficult to tap into your inner creative well? Do you find your not-self emotion of anger showing up in those places or with those people more often?
3. How do you feel about informing others of what you're doing? Keep in mind that informing is for you to create more ease in your life, *not* to ask permission for what you're about to do. It's a courtesy to the people around you.
4. How do you allow yourself to be powerful? Where in your life do you shy away from your power? Are there physical implications of restraining your power or keeping yourself playing it small? Do you have any physical pains or chronic issues that you've noticed in regard to saying no when you want to say yes to initiating?
5. What holds you back from fulfilling your potential?
6. What have you created in your life? What are some of your proudest accomplishments? What was your creative process like in those experiences?
7. How are you at delegating or handing over tasks for others to finish or help with?
8. How do you feel about your sense of personal worthiness of love, affection, and connection?

In this last set of questions, we will explore your *parenting* experience as a Manifestor.

1. How do you inform your family about what you plan to do when you need time to focus?
2. How do you inform your children or partner what will happen where you are concerned? I.e., do you tell them when you are going to be away for an extended period of time? Do you inform them of what you need them to do in order

to get out of the house on time for school, or if the family dynamics are going to change, for example?

3. What role does anger play in your parenting? How often does it show up? How do you handle it? Do you deny it or own up to it and talk about what happened and apologize if it comes out directed at someone? How do you hold yourself accountable for the changes you say you'll make when you find yourself apologizing? Something to remember here is that an apology that never comes often hurts worse than an apology from a parent who is trying and doesn't always get it right, but who keeps taking action to make it better. We don't always get it right the first time. How do you allow yourself grace around this concept?
4. How does anger make you feel as a parent? What judgments do you have about feeling anger?
5. How does anger show up when your kids or partner interrupt you?
6. What would you like your family to know and understand about you and your anger? Imagine for a moment that you and your anger are in a personal relationship. How would you describe your relationship with anger to them? How do you help one another? How do you talk about one another? Does anger judge you? Do you judge anger? How could you be in a better relationship with anger?
7. If your child were struggling with anger as their not-self emotion, what would you do or say to support them? What does your inner child need to hear about the role anger plays in your life?
8. How are your kids similar or different from you in regard to anger? If they are emotionally undefined, do they amplify and express anger too?
9. What words or phrases do you hear come out of your mouth in your parenting that leave you a little stunned and sound like a parent figure you grew up with? How does that make you feel toward yourself and/or your child? What would you want to be different?
10. What are your favorite things you learned about parenting through your parents?

These questions are for parents of any energy type with a Manifestor energy type child. So, if you are a Manifestor, Manifesting Generator, Generator, Projector, or Reflector, and you have a Manifestor child, this section is for you.

MANIFESTOR CHILD

What Parents Need to Learn about Their Manifestor Children

1. It is important to inform them of the things that will affect them, what you expect of them, etc.
2. You'll need to give them a window of time to complete tasks, let them choose when to initiate doing them within that window, and inform them of the consequences of not completing them ahead of time.
3. Start to teach them to inform you of what they plan to do. This will become a courtesy to you later on, as it's not really about asking permission with Manifestors.
4. They need cycles of rest; they're not lazy. They just need to be resourced before they initiate the next thing.
5. The harder you try to control them, the more they're likely to rebel.
6. Don't condition their initiating spark out of them or teach them to be people pleasers.
7. Emotional Manifestors need time to make decisions.

What a Manifestor Child Needs, and Needs to Learn

1. **About their magic**—They need to learn that their imagination and inner creative drive *are* their magic.
2. **To inform**—They need to inform others who need to know or will be affected by what they plan to do. When they're young, this has a lot of benefits for the parent to be able to screen for things that are unsafe, but as they grow, this is not about asking permission but informing others of what they are going to do.

We want to teach our young Manifestors that they don't need to ask permission to follow that inner creative drive, so they don't suppress it, but at the same time, we have to be aware of what they plan on doing (when younger) so they don't hurt themselves or others with their inventions or ideas.

Your being informed and their being able to explore and create in this way as much as possible not only nourishes this innate part of them, but also it encourages them to tell you what they plan on doing before they do it. If they grow up feeling like they aren't allowed to follow this inner creative drive without punishment or being shut down all the time, they will likely create a secret part of their life, where they do things they feel called to do without telling you.

What I notice is that around age eleven or twelve, if Manifestor children have not had a parent who understood their initiating nature and how they are different in this regard, they start to push back. They argue more, express anger more easily, and test their parents. This is not a judgment of the parents, just an observation of the authentic self of the Manifestor trying to emerge and the parent doing what they have known to do.

While the Manifestor is only 8-9 percent of the population, I have rarely seen multiple Manifestors in one nuclear family, and considering that they need to be parented differently, this is a common time for those growing pains to emerge as they become preteen/teens and are looking for more autonomy in their lives.

3. **Support**—They need parents or someone in their life who will take their hand when they dream up big ideas and say, "Let's see how that works!" or "Show me!" They need someone who allows them to lead and take them on a journey of what it is for them to manifest something they feel called to create. They need to be able to dream and explore.
4. **To be informed**—They need to be informed of things that will affect them. Remember, this could be anything from working late, to moving to another home, bringing someone new into their lives, or expecting their chores to be completed by a certain time.
5. **Cycles of initiating and rest**—They need to learn to work in cycles that allow them to create and have time to rest. When they're tired, they need to recharge.

6. **Different energy patterns**—They need to learn that they don't have the same level of renewable energy that a Generator or Manifesting Generator has and to build in downtime in their life.

7. **Right work**—When they grow up, working a nine-to-five day might not be right for them. They need to find work that aligns with their energy pattern and that they feel inspired to do where they can bring their new ideas to share. Alternatively, they might find one career that they stick with that allows them to create in waves as well, such as graphic design or architecture, restoring old cars, or anything else where they can draw on their creativity and then initiate it. They could even be accountants or spreadsheet wizards creating things that save the rest of us who don't love to work with numbers time and energy.

8. **Grace**—They need to know that they won't be punished for being someone who is driven to follow their inner creative drive.

9. **Open-ended questions**—They need you to ask them open-ended questions such as: What do you think about ____? How do you feel about ____? Tell me more about ____.

10. **Emotional Authority—**They need to learn to give themselves time to make big decisions. See Emotional Authority in chapter four, for more details.

Journal Prompts for a Parent with a Manifestor Child

1. How do you let your Manifestor lead or initiate? Can you identify any ways that keep your Manifestor from being allowed to follow their inner creative drive?

2. Do you recognize the signature emotion of anger in your Manifestor child? Do you see it often? If so, how do you support them with it? If not, write about a time when their anger exploded and how you navigated that. Then write about how you see the situation through the lens of Human Design, knowing that your child is a Manifestor and what you might try next time.

3. Do you have any judgments about their not-self emotion of anger? Do you feel differently about it when it's just the two of your versus when you're in public or around friends or family?
4. How has understanding the Manifestor energy type helped you to see your child as a unique individual? How has it helped you to parent them? What challenges do you still struggle with?
5. What ideals have you held about how children should behave that have been challenged by parenting your Manifestor? Are there any parenting strategies that you're ready to let go of that are not working for parenting your Manifestor child? What might still need some more time to shift in your parenting?
6. Do other family members have strong ideas about how you should parent your Manifestor? If so, how do they affect how you allow yourself to parent your Manifestor child?

Generators

Sacral Energy Type—Approximately 70 Percent of the Population

Purpose: Workforce builders. To find proficiency in their work by responding to what life brings them through their Strategy or responding.

Strategy: To wait for something to show up in their external reality and then respond through their Sacral response.

Signature Emotion: Satisfaction

Signature Not-Self Emotion: Frustration

Generators are here to be part of the workforce/life force/builders and doers of the world. Though they are here with this beautiful, renewable energy source and can do more physical work than non-sacral energy types, they are not here to do all the stuff no one else wants to do. They will find proficiency in their work by responding to what life brings them through their Strategy. Over time they become very good at the art of working—in whatever work they do that they've responded to through their Sacral response.

Generators learn through a stair-step learning pattern. When they are on a plateau, it is very tempting for them to jump ship and move on to something else. It is important for this energy type to learn to quit things correctly as well.

As a Generator, you are designed to respond to what life brings you, but you must be connected to your Sacral response and aligned with your truth. If you aren't connected to this inner knowing of what's right for you, you may take on things that deplete your energy and say no to things that you really enjoy. Complete only the questions you feel aligned with and are called to answer. You may find you want to come back at another time and feel called to answer other questions you initially left blank, and that's okay. This is your journey, and you can choose how you approach it.

A Quick Reminder of What Generator Parents Need to Learn

(For more details, reference chapter five in *Parenting the Child You Have,* the book)

1. **To follow your Sacral response**—Getting and staying connected to your Sacral response helps you to navigate what is correct for you and is how you will make parenting decisions that are correct for you. Without this connection, you can begin to rely on your mind to make decisions, which is not the source of your truth; your mind can, however, be helpful in planning and strategizing once you've committed to something. As a Generator you must first align with your yes/no response to know that when you respond, it is correct for you.
2. **To learn to say no and follow your yeses**—Just as important as learning to say yes to the things that light up your Sacral Center, you must learn how to say no to the things that are incorrect for you. In parenting, this can be where you step out of the societal norm and choose to parent in your way, since you feel in your gut that it's right—or not—for you.
3. **To quit the people-pleasing**—Just because you have the energy (or can find the energy) to do all of the things that others don't really want to do doesn't mean you should. Caretaking and being supportive can be one way a Generator

parent or partner can show love and affection, but it's important to know when you're taking on more than your fair share. This is also an opportunity to not only practice boundaries but to teach your children and family that just because you can doesn't mean you always will.

4. **To not initiate**—Remember, life will send you everything you need. You just need to listen and respond through your Sacral response. To be clear, you can begin once you've responded to something external. If you dream up a great idea, wait for a sign or something to respond to that the timing is right for you. Then check in with your Sacral to see if it's correct for you or if it's an idea that's meant for someone else to bring into form.
5. **To not do everything for your non-Sacral family**—Because you have a more easily renewed source of energy, Generator parents can tend to be the ones who take on a lot of the household chores and tasks because it's easier to do them than to keep asking or telling your non-sacral family they need doing. Learn to ask your family in the way that is correct for them. Ask your Projectors to help out and then recognize the good work they do. When they feel recognized, they'll more willingly help out again. Inform your Manifestors what needs to be done and give them a time frame for them to choose when they will do it. Your Reflectors can get on board and match your energy for a while if they've had proper rest, so make it fun!
6. **To give decisions time if you have Emotional Authority**—You need to connect and listen to your Sacral Authority and then give your big decisions time. If you're making a decision about your family, as in where to live, a change of jobs, or a big decision that will affect your children, make sure you wait out the highs and lows of your wave and make a decision when you're feeling somewhere in the middle of your wave. See the Emotional Authority section in chapter four for more on this.
7. **Finding your way**—You may need to try some things and explore what works for you. Your Sacral may say yes to trying something, but it may not end up being a long-term solution. Don't judge yourself. Recognize when your Sacral *yes*, turns to a Sacral *no* and be willing to change directions and try something else.

8. **Use your energy**—As a Generator you need to use your physical energy each day. If you are too sedentary, you can have difficulty focusing, feeling settled, and managing your emotions, (like frustration, the not-self signature emotion). Physical movement to the level that feels good and settles your energy each day is important and will help you remain more patient as a parent.

Journal Prompts for Generator Parents

Before we begin, let's check to see if now is a good time for you to explore journaling about being a Generator parent. Do you want to do this exercise and exploration right now? If yes, please continue on. If no, please skip this lesson until your Sacral response says yes.

First, we will explore your *childhood* experience as a Generator

1. Were you praised for all the things you accomplished as a child? If so, write about how you felt receiving praise for getting things done. If not, is there anything you'd like to explore around this topic? If so, spend a few minutes journaling about it.
2. Were you allowed to explore different ways of doing tasks so you could find *your* way? Whether you did or did not, how did this shape how you approach tasks and things now as an adult?
3. Did you regularly move your body as a child? Were you encouraged to play sports or other forms of movement? Write about your experience moving your body and your energy needs as a child. Is it similar or different compared to when you were a child?
4. Were you raised by non-sacral parents? If so, did you feel judged for not being able to be calmer?
5. Were you labeled as ADD or ADHD as a child whether through official diagnosis or just referenced to them due to your high energy? If so, do you feel this was accurate or perhaps related to your unreleased energy levels as a Generator?

6. Were you allowed space to wait for life to give you things to respond to as a child, or were you expected to take initiative on things before being asked?
7. Do you remember what things lit you up or excited you as a child? What were your favorite things to do?
8. What things did you really dislike and not want to do as a child? Did you have to do them anyway? Do you still dislike them? What did you learn?
9. How did you express your excitement?

Next, we will explore your *adulthood* as a Generator

1. Do you wait to respond, or do you jump in and take action before being asked?
2. Do you wait for something to show up in life to respond to rather than trying to force things to happen? Write about what you notice around your tendencies to wait or jump in.
3. Are you doing what you envisioned your adult self to be doing when you were a child?
4. Do you remember what you wanted to be when you were five? Twelve? Seventeen? If so, write them down. How do you feel about them now?
5. Are there responsibilities you have taken on as an adult that you don't like doing? If so, what are they?
6. Would it feel good to let go of the responsibilities or things you're doing with your energy that you don't enjoy? If so, what is one thing you could stop doing today to free up your energy for more of what you enjoy doing?
7. Do you know what you would like to do more of? If so, what? If not, set a timer for five minutes and just start writing down whatever comes to mind. Don't edit, don't proofread, and don't consider anyone else. Just write what is true for you at this moment. Then look back upon what you wrote after the five minutes and see what you notice.
8. Do you listen to your gut when making decisions?

9. Do you feel positive about your worthiness of love, affection, and connection? If yes, what is one piece of advice you would give to someone else struggling with this? If not, what areas would you like to work on?
10. How do you move your body to use your energy daily? What happens when you don't get enough exercise?
11. Do you allow yourself the gift of time in making decisions to honor your Emotional Authority (if you have one)?

In this last set of questions, we will explore your *parenting* as a Generator

1. Do you clean up after your kids, or do you allow them/make/encourage them to clean up after themselves?
2. If you're always cleaning up after everyone else, how do you feel about it? Do you feel appreciated and valued?
3. Do you have Generator/Manifesting Generator kids or Projector, Manifestor, or Reflector kids? How do you parent them to stay true to themselves?
4. Are your kids more similar or different from you?
5. Are there any words that you hear pop out of your mouth that sound like a parent figure you grew up with that leave you feeling a little stunned? How does that make you feel toward yourself or your child?
6. When your child gets frustrated with a task, do you let them work their process to figure it out (unless they ask for help), or do you preemptively jump in and fix it or solve the problem for them?
7. Have you ever felt burned out? If so, do you know what helps you recover?
8. Do you feel burned out now? If so, what are some things you're saying yes to that you'd like to say no to?

These questions are for parents of any energy type with a Generator energy type child. So, if you are a Manifestor, Manifesting Generator, Projector, or Reflector, and you have a Generator child, this section is for you.

GENERATOR CHILD

What Parents Need to Learn about Their Generator Children

1. **Physical energy needs**—Make sure your child expends their physical energy each day so they can properly rest at night. Contrary to what we tend to be taught, if a Generator or Manifesting Generator child is wound up before bed, it's actually more beneficial to find something for them to do to use up that physical energy than try to fight it and make them try and go to sleep. Trampolines, jumping jacks, dancing, or anything that uses up that energy and wears them out will help get them into bed and get you that quiet time for yourself after they're asleep.
2. **Teach them to honor their no**—Teach your children that it's okay to say no. We want our Generator children to grow up connected to their Sacral response and not ignore it to do what others want them to do. One of the most important things they need to learn is how to listen to their noes and be able to have them heard. If they learn to ignore their Sacral *no*, they stop listening to what is best for them and can end up living a life of people-pleasing. It's important to teach them about their Sacral response and know that it's different from a no that comes from the conditioned mind. If they have Emotional Authority, ask them again later and see if the response stays the same. We'll cover the inner authorities more in chapter four.
3. **To trust their gut**—Teach your children to listen to their gut and trust it.
4. **Ask them yes/no questions**—Their Sacral response works best when they have a yes/no or this/that type of question. Open-ended questions confuse their Sacral response, and they end up trying to figure out the "right" answer with their minds. This is not correct for them. It's actually not correct for any of us to use our minds to make decisions. While they can make a great outer authority for others and help us strategize, organize, and approach things once we've

decided they are right for us, they are not for making the decision to move forward with an invitation or something to respond to.

What a Generator Child Needs and Needs to Learn

1. **To trust their gut**—They can trust their gut knowing. Help them connect to that innate knowing that lives in their belly and speaks to them through sound. Listen to the sounds that come out of them. Do they say yes/no, or uh-huh/unh-uh, or yep/nope? What does their yes and no sound like? Listen for it and learn to trust them so that they can continue to trust this knowing within themselves.

2. **To speak up for their noes**—They need to know they can say no when their gut tells them no. This one can be harder for parents because sometimes you've gone to a lot of effort to arrange something for them, or you've paid for expensive lessons and bought the uniforms or costumes for them. But when their bodies are saying no, and we try to convince them to do it anyway, we teach them not to listen to the voice within that guides them. We teach them to question themselves and that they aren't capable of making good decisions. We have to decide if it's more important to teach them to honor their truth or ours. I love to imagine a world where we feel so confident in ourselves and our ability to make good decisions that we don't have to try and get others to do what *we* think is best for them rather than what *they* think is best for them.

3. **They don't have to do it all**—They do not have to do all the work that no one else wants to do. If your child is in a family or a group of people who do not have defined Sacral Centers for example, the Generator child can be the one who tends to feel obligated to pick up the slack and carry the weight of doing the work when it's not a desirable task. Help them to get comfortable trusting their gut yes/no and speaking up for what they need. They can invite others to help them or ask for someone to take on specific tasks so that they aren't left trying to do all the things, especially the things that aren't as fun.

4. **Move their bodies**—They need to move their bodies daily for optimal health. Help them learn that if they are having trouble concentrating they might need to move their body more. Ask them questions in the evening about their energy level and how ready they feel for sleep so that they start to connect their energy level and what they need to be able to rest properly. Ask them if they'd like to

go for a walk or dance to their favorite song or something similar if they need to expend more energy before sleep.

5. **Wait to respond**—They must wait for things to respond to, but life will bring them every opportunity they need. Teach them that they are not Manifestors and that all they have to do is be present and listen and watch. The world will bring them all kinds of opportunities to respond to, and they can choose which ones are correct for them. If they have an Emotional Authority, they need to give themselves more time for the bigger decisions. Inner Authority is covered in more detail in chapter four.

Journal Prompts for a Parent of a Generator Child

1. Do you listen to your Generator child when they tell you they want to stop classes, end friendships, not hug certain family members, etc.? If the answer is no, what internal story is playing within you that keeps you from allowing them to quit? Get quiet and listen, does the voice you hear sound like yours or someone else's? Do you know whose voice it is? What would happen if you challenged that voice?

2. Does your child have excess energy at the end of the day? If so, how much movement are they getting in their day? How can you find ways to help them get more? If they go to sleep easily and stay asleep, what are you doing to help them release their energy during the day?

3. Are you a Sacral energy type or a non-Sacral energy type? How does that affect parenting your Generator child? If you are a non-Sacral type, do you find parenting exhausting? Do you find it energizing? How do you take time for yourself? If you are a Sacral energy type, do you feel like you've deconditioned enough around your energy type to teach your Sacral energy child how to live an aligned life? If so, what is the most important thing you've taught them about being a Generator or Manifesting Generator? If not, what do you need to heal, release, or align within yourself to be a good example of living an aligned life as a Generator or Manifesting Generator?

4. If you are a Generator, what is your biggest childhood wound around your energy type? How has that shaped your adult life? How can you best support your child to discontinue that pattern?
5. What role does frustration play in your child's learning? How do you navigate it when frustration arises? Do you let them experience their frustration, or do you try to suppress it? Do you feel judgment from family or others about your child's frustration? How does that affect your parenting?

Manifesting Generators

Sacral Energy Type—Approximately 35 Percent of the Population

Purpose: Workforce builders. To find proficiency in their work by responding to what life brings them through their Strategy.

Strategy: To wait for something to show up in their external reality and inform those who will be impacted by their actions.

Signature Emotion: Satisfaction

Signature Not-Self Emotion: Frustration and anger

As a Manifesting Generator, you are here to do many things, often simultaneously. You are a Generator type at your core with some additional qualities, such as being able to act quickly through your Sacral response in taking action once you've responded to something external to you. This is the key here. Often times, Manifesting Generators mistakenly think that because they have a lot of energy and the capacity to act quickly, that they can think things up and make them happen, but they still need to wait for something external to them to show up that they respond to with their Sacral sounds, the uh-huh, unh-uh.

You can cultivate skill in many things in your lifetime, and you teach us where we can skip steps through your experiential learning. Due to this learning style, you may find yourself repeating steps because you have sped through them without waiting. This is not a problem necessarily— it's your way of learning by doing. You learn through a stair-step learning pattern. When you are on a plateau, it is very tempting for you to jump ship and move on to something else. It is important to learn to quit things correctly for your energy type as well. Just as your Sacral response can tell you when to engage in an activity or task, it can also tell you when you're done with the task. If you are not clear on your yes/no, I suggest having a Sacral session to help you get to your innate knowing without your mind jumping in to say, "I'm bored with this right now. I quit." You might be on the edge of greatness and just need to wait a little longer or gather more skills, resources, or people to help you get to the next level or step.

You may have been told you're flighty or can't stick with one thing. That is not true. You're designed to move on when you've gotten what you need from a process. But there is that big caveat about knowing when and how to quit correctly rather than just ping-ponging around following your mind and all the shiny things. This is the biggest thing I see Manifesting Generators need help deconditioning in their lives. They either quit too soon, or they hang on too long. Correctly quitting is an art that you need to learn as a Manifesting Generator.

A Quick Reminder of What Manifesting Generator Parents Need to Learn

(For more details, reference chapter five in *Parenting the Child You Have,* the book)

1. **To follow your Sacral response**—Getting and staying connected to your Sacral response helps you to navigate what is correct for you and is also how you will make parenting decisions that are correct for you. Without this connection, you rely on your mind to make decisions, which is not the source of your truth. While the mind can be helpful in planning and strategizing, as a Manifesting Generator, you must first align with your yes/no response to know that when you respond, it is correct for you.
2. **To learn to say no and follow your yeses—**Just as important as learning to say yes to the things that light up your Sacral Center, you must learn how to say no to the things that are incorrect for you.

   In parenting, this can be where you step out of the societal norm and choose to parent in your own way, since you feel in your gut that it's right—or not—for you.

3. **To quit people-pleasing**—Just because you have the energy (or can find the energy) to do all of the things that others don't really want to do doesn't mean you should. Caretaking and being supportive can be one way a Manifesting Generator parent or partner can show love and affection, but it's important to know when you're taking on more than your fair share. This is also an opportunity to not only practice boundaries but also to teach your children and family that just because you can doesn't mean you always will.

4. **To not initiate until you've responded to something external, then inform those who will be affected**—Remember, life will send you everything you need. You just need to listen and respond through your Sacral response. To be clear, you can begin once you've responded to something external to you. If you dream up a great idea, wait for a sign or something to respond to that the timing is right for you. Then check in with your Sacral to see if it's correct for you or an idea that's meant for someone else to bring into form. Then inform anyone who will be affected by your action.

5. **To inform once your Sacral response says yes**—The manifesting part of the Manifesting Generator needs you to inform others of what you plan to do so you are not interrupted in your process.

6. **To not do everything for your non-Sacral family**—Because you have a more easily renewed source of energy, as a Manifesting Generator parent you can tend to be the one who takes on a lot of the household chores and tasks because it's easier to just do them than to keep asking or telling your non-Sacral family they need doing. Learn to ask your family in the way that is correct for them. Ask your Projectors to help out and then recognize the good work they do. When they feel recognized, they'll more willingly help out again. Inform your Manifestors what needs to be done and give them a time frame to choose when they will do it. Your Reflectors can get on board and match your energy for a while if they've had proper rest, so make it fun!

7. **Finding your way**—You may need to try some things and explore what works for you. Your Sacral may respond yes to trying something, but it may not end up being a long-term solution. Don't judge yourself. Recognize when your

Sacral yes turns to a Sacral no and be willing to change directions and try something else.

8. **Use your energy**—Manifesting Generators need to use their physical energy each day. If you are too sedentary, you can have difficulty focusing, feeling settled, and managing your emotions, like frustration (your not-self signature emotion). Physical movement to the level that feels good and settles your energy each day is important and will help you remain more patient as a parent.
9. **To give decisions time if you have Emotional Authority**—You need to connect and listen to your Sacral Authority and then give your big decisions time. If you're making a decision about your family, such as where to live, a change of jobs, or a big decision that will affect your children, make sure you wait out the highs and lows of your wave and make a decision when you're feeling somewhere in the middle of your wave. See the Emotional Authority section in chapter four for more on this.
10. **Being multi-passionate**—You are designed to do multiple things simultaneously. This is great for you. However, if you have a child who is not a Manifesting Generator, make sure to honor what they need and do not expect them to mirror your actions if you want them to stay in alignment with their own energy.

Journal Prompts for Manifesting Generator Parents

Before we begin, let's check to see if now is a good time for you to explore journaling about being a Manifesting Generator parent. Do you want to do this exercise and exploration right now? If yes, please continue. If no, please skip this lesson until your Sacral response says yes.

First, we will explore your *childhood* experience as a Manifesting Generator

1. Were you told that you couldn't stick with things growing up? (Sports, music, dance, etc.)
2. Did you feel like others relied on you to get things done?

3. Did you ever feel guilty for daydreaming and not being productive?
4. How many projects did you have going at one time?
5. Were you allowed to try and fail and try again?
6. Were you a color-one-page-at-a-time kid, or a try-out-a-little-of-one-page-until-you-got-bored-and-jumped-to-something-else kid? Were you allowed to jump around and not finish everything you started?

Next, we will explore your *adulthood* as a Manifesting Generator

1. How many careers or different jobs have you had?
2. Do you have any judgments about the quantity or variety of careers or jobs you've had?
3. Are you often told that you jump from thing to thing? Is it okay for you to jump from thing to thing?
4. Do you listen to your gut when making decisions?
5. Do you feel good about your worthiness of love, affection, and connection? If not, write about your feelings.
6. Would you choose to explore more careers or paths in life if you knew no one would judge you for changing directions again?

In this last set of questions, we will explore your *parenting* as a Manifesting Generator

1. Are your kids similar or different from you? How?
2. What words do you hear pop out of your mouth that sound like a parent figure you grew up with that leave you a little stunned? How does that make you feel toward yourself and your child?
3. Do you inform your child of what to expect before or after you've changed the rules, family dynamics, or anything else that will affect them?
4. Do you and your child argue or experience conflict? Around what areas/topics?
5. How do you honor your child's energy needs? If not, why?

These questions are for parents of any energy type with a Manifesting Generator energy type child. So, if you are a Manifestor, Generator, Projector, or Reflector, and you have a Manifesting Generator child, this section is for you.

MANIFESTING GENERATOR CHILD

What Parents Need to Learn about Their Manifesting Generator Children

1. **Skipping steps is okay**—It's okay and normal for them to skip steps; however, they will often have to go back and repeat steps. Let them. Do not shame them for going too fast or skipping steps that you would have taken. They are still learning this process, which is about trial and error, figuring out when to skip steps or not. Let them know it's okay to do it their way.
2. **Multi-taskers**—They are designed to do many things at once. Within budget and time constraints, let them try many things. The more experiences they have, the more they gather knowledge about what they like and don't and how they want to use their energy.
3. **Go all in**—They need to commit to things fully (even if they don't pan out or they change direction). This means listening to their inner Authority when engaging in a project, task, relationship, sport, or other commitment. If they don't go all in, they won't know if it didn't work out because they didn't give it enough time and energy, or if they just got bored or were low-key committed to too many things at once. Though they have that beautiful renewable energy source through their defined Sacral Centers, there is still a limit to how much energy they generate in a day.
4. **Quit correctly**—They need to quit correctly. (Is their Sacral telling them that they're done with things, or do they let their mind or others decide?) Help teach them to understand and rely on their inner Authority. We'll cover inner Authority in chapter four.
5. **Let them work it out**—They have their own process for working, and sometimes they'll have to repeat steps. That's okay. Normal even. Learn to embrace it.

6. **They're not flighty—**They are not being flighty for not sticking with decisions when they quit things correctly. They just need to quit correctly for their energy Type and Authority.

What a Manifesting Generator Child Needs and Needs to Learn

1. **Multi-task**—It's okay to be doing many things at one time.
2. **Quit (correctly)**—It's okay to quit when they are done with something. (Teach them to quit correctly through their Sacral response.)
3. **Move their bodies**—They need to move their bodies daily for optimal health.
4. **Pivot!**—It's okay to change directions in their interests or later on in careers as their Sacral leads them on their life's journey in response to opportunities.
5. **To inform—**After they've responded with their Sacral response, they need to inform anyone who will be affected by what they are going to do.

Journal Prompts for a Parent with a Manifesting Generator Child

1. Do you listen to your Manifesting Generator child when they tell you they want to stop classes, end friendships, not hug certain family members, etc.?
2. Does your child have an excess of energy at the end of the day? If so, how much movement are they getting in their day? How can you find ways to help them get more? If they go to sleep easily and stay asleep, what are you doing to help them expend their energy each day?
3. Do you allow your child to quit sports, classes, hobbies, etc., when they tell you they are done with it and don't want to pursue them anymore?
4. What does it mean to you that your child jumps from interest to interest regularly?
5. What attachments do you have around their future career?
6. What role does frustration play in your child's learning? How do you navigate it when frustration arises?

Projectors

Non-Sacral Energy Type—Approximately 20 Percent of the Population

Purpose: To guide

Strategy: To wait for an invitation to the big things in life and to wait for the right timing to share their insights with others after being recognized.

Signature Emotion: Success

Signature Not-Self Emotion: Bitterness

Projectors are here to help guide energy. They can see the bigger picture from a 40,000-foot view and offer guidance that saves time, energy, and effort, but their guidance *must* be invited. When they offer their insight or guidance without being invited to do so, they can meet resistance, disagreement, defensiveness, or avoidance, which can hurt the Projector who just wants to help. This can lead the Projector to feel their signature emotion of bitterness when they don't feel like they are living out their purpose. They can also feel bitterness when they are tired, which often stems from them overdoing it physically, trying to prove their value, or creating invitations.

Projectors find success when they stop pushing with their energy, offering advice and guidance without an invitation and instead focus on doing what they enjoy and wait for a true invitation to come to them. The invitation must have the recognition that is unique to them rather than an invitation that anyone can fill. When the Projector is seen for who they are and what they can offer, the invitation can feel magical and is the currency of their soul. Though they may receive a personal invitation, it is up to the Projector to use their inner Authority to know if the invitation is correct for them. Just because they have been invited and feel recognized does not mean it's automatically a correct invitation for them, and they must be wise about the invitations they accept. Waiting and passing up on incorrect invitations can be incredibly difficult at the beginning of their deconditioning because it can sometimes take a very long time for a correct invitation to come along. The more bitterness a Projector feels, the fewer invitations they receive, so remember to encourage Projectors to find their joy from within, and the invitations will begin to flow.

Projector children need you to recognize what they are good at and verbalize it. Let them know what they're good at and where they excel. Remember that what they excel at may not look the same as other energy types. Rather than being great at remembering to do their chores, a Projector may be really great at organizing a bookshelf for you or helping you to put your list of to-do items in an order that saves you trips out or running around. Remember, they guide energy. They are not the workforce energy of the planet and praising them to do and work in the typical way we think of work, conditions them away from their energetic alignment and can lead to burnout in adulthood if they do not correct the pattern.

A Quick Reminder of What Projector Parents Need to Learn

(For more details, reference chapter five in *Parenting the Child You Have,* the book)

1. **Energy**—You don't have the same level of renewable energy as 70 percent of the population, so learning to parent in *your way* is crucial.
2. **Breaks**—You need regular breaks to use your energy wisely.
3. **Self-nourishment**—You need to do things that nourish you, away from the kids.
4. **Self-value**—Bitterness means you're tired or not valuing yourself. Do things your way and stop trying to keep up with others.
5. **Invitations**—Invitations will not be plentiful if you don't value yourself.
6. **Sounding boards—**You need people around you who can be your sounding boards, rather than give advice.

Journal Prompts for Projector Parents

First, we will explore your *childhood* experience as a Projector

1. Were you raised in a Generator or Manifesting Generator dominant family? If so, how did that affect your perception of energy?
2. What did you most like to do as a child when you were alone?

3. What did you find yourself doing in groups that you did or didn't enjoy?
4. What was your experience with childhood friendships?
5. What was your relationship to doing physical work?
6. How did you feel about fairness growing up?
7. What did you get recognized for as a child?
8. Were you ever or often told you were bossy? If so, how might that have prevented you from guiding as a Projector?

Next, we will explore your *adulthood* as a Projector

1. How have you experienced relationships as a Projector before and after learning about Human Design?
2. Have you burned out? What was that like? What led to it?
3. Do you feel burned out now? What do you feel would help you recover? If you have healed from burnout, what did it take for you to heal?
4. If you have burned out and recovered, what did you learn about yourself? What were the physical sensations, diagnoses, or other ailments that you had during that time?
5. If you have not healed from burnout and are in it now, do you know what you need to heal?
6. Are there things in your life that you're doing out of obligation but could let go of? If so, how would it feel to let go of doing all the things you feel like you *should* be doing?
7. What is your relationship with work now as an adult?
8. What do you value about yourself in the work you do? Is it aligned with your inherent Projector energy?
9. Do you recognize your bitterness when it shows up? What does it tell you? How do you navigate it?

In this last set of questions, we will explore your *parenting* as a Projector

1. How are your kids similar or different from you?
2. What energy struggles do you experience as a Projector parent?
3. If you have Sacral energy children (Generators and Manifesting Generators), how do you get them enough exercise to wear themselves out without exhausting yourself?
4. How do you find time to do the things you enjoy and make yourself feel fulfilled?
5. What words do you hear pop out of your mouth and sound like a parent figure you grew up with that leave you a little stunned? How does that make you feel toward yourself and your child?
6. How do you feel about your worthiness of love, affection, and connection?
7. How are you allowing yourself proper rest?
8. Do you allow others, i.e., children and partners, to take care of the things they are capable of, or do you feel like you should be doing it for them because you are the parent or spouse?
9. What do you do to encourage your children to do age-appropriate tasks for themselves rather than rely on you for everything as their parent?
10. Who are your sounding boards? How do they help you get clarity?

These questions are for parents of any energy type with a Projector energy type child. So, if you are a Manifestor, Manifesting Generator, Generator, Projector, or Reflector, and you have a Projector child, this section is for you.

PROJECTOR CHILD

What Parents Need to Learn about Their Projector Children

1. **They need to be recognized and invited**—Sometimes, you will have to facilitate the invitation for them to friendships, parties, events, jobs, career paths, etc.
2. **Processing thoughts and feelings**—They often need to process their decisions verbally to know how they think or feel about something. They may need to revisit the same topic many times to get clarity, and they need you to let them come to their own understanding. Hold space and ask them thought-provoking and open-ended questions, refraining from giving advice unless asked. Even when asked, it's better to help them think critically about their own answer than give them yours, as you'll teach them to trust themselves.
3. **Emotional Authority**—They need to spend time with their feelings before making a big decision. It can feel like a very long time to wait for parents or people with a quick inner Authority such as Sacral or Splenic.
4. **Friendships can be difficult**—They need your support through the hard times and help to learn that the right friendships make them feel valued.
5. **They need downtime to recharge**—Especially if they grow up in a Generator/Manifesting Generator household, they need help recognizing that though they can take in and amplify the Sacral energy around them, it's not sustainable, and relying on it can lead to burnout later in life. Help them learn to listen to their body's needs.
6. **They can be bossy**—If they don't have enough invitations to share what they know, they can start telling others what they know or how they should do things differently. Try and create enough opportunities for your Projectors to share what they know or to contribute.

What a Projector Child Needs and Needs to Learn

1. **Wait to share**—They need to learn to wait to share their knowledge until asked for the best reception by others.
2. **A good invitation**—What a good invitation is for a Projector. It must be one where they feel recognized, and it must be specific to them.
3. **Proper rest**—They must rest properly so they don't end up in burnout by age thirty.
4. **Sounding boards**—They need to have people who allow them to verbally process without giving advice and to value those people.
5. **Friendships**—They may know a lot of people, but they will have a few close friendships that they must be invited into.
6. **Personal pursuit of their passions does not need an invitation**—They can pursue their interests without an invitation unless it involves someone else's participation.
7. **When an invitation is needed**—Invitations are for the big things in life—career, love, friendships, and where to live.
8. **Bitterness**—That *they* are not bitter, but that bitterness is a sign that something is out of alignment for them. Are they tired? Are they pushing and not waiting for an invitation? Are they not feeling recognized?

Journal Prompts for a Parent with a Projector Child

1. How do you recognize your Projector child for their gifts, talents, and uniqueness?
2. Do you make a habit of setting time aside each day to ask your Projector child what is on their mind, heart, or other?
3. How do you handle bossiness from your Projector? What have you learned about navigating bossiness from a Projector? Are they getting enough recognition, or are they pushing for it with their bossiness?
4. Do you ask your Projector child open-ended questions? Are you a Sacral energy type or a non-Sacral energy type? If you're a Sacral energy type, how do you practice slowing down and allowing your Projector child the space to process their thoughts and feelings?
5. If you are a Sacral energy type, how do you feel about waiting? How can you practice more patience while waiting for your non-Sacral child to process their responses to your questions?
6. Do you allow your Projector child downtime to unwind before bed and encourage them to listen to their body's needs when it needs to slow down and rest?
7. How do you allow yourself to be their sounding board rather than give advice? Or who are their sounding boards that they go to for clarity on processing their decisions and thoughts?

Reflectors

Non-Sacral Energy Type—Approximately 1 Percent of the Population

Focus on Who You Are BEing, Not How Much You Are DOing

Purpose: To reflect the health and status of the community

Strategy: To wait through a lunar cycle before making a big decision

Signature Emotion: Surprise

Signature Not-Self Emotion: Disappointment

Reflectors are here to find true delight in the world around them through the environments and experiences they find themselves in. We often talk about how the Reflector is the barometer of the world and tells us more about what is going on within their environment; and true, this is what the rest of us get from them. But that doesn't really tell the Reflector about what they get out of living this life of reflection for others. They are individuals with needs, wants, desires, likes, and dislikes, just like everyone else. Time alone is critical for them to not only discharge the energy they pick up from others in their day-to-day life but also to sit in their own energy and consider who they are and what they want.

Ideally, they need to be taught from a young age to sample the energy of the people and environments around them and not take them on as their own. They are learning from their surroundings and the people around them, but they aren't designed to take it on as their identity, as this can create a lot of pain and confusion in the Reflector. They need to have safe people to talk to about their decisions as they take their lunar cycle to come to their decisions. Providing a safe space for them to be who they are (especially when that is ever-changing) while trying out all the flavors of what life has to offer, is very important for them. The disappointment that they can experience is a reflection of what is happening around them and how the world and the people around them are not living up to the potential the Reflector knows is possible. With encouragement, they can grow up to be people who don't attach deeply to behavior that they see in others and allow space to be delighted in who others can be when they live in alignment. They can dance with your delight or disappointment, so if you don't like what you see in your Reflector, remember to look around and back at yourself to see what they may be mirroring.

A Quick Reminder of What Reflector Parents Need to Learn

(For more details, reference chapter five in *Parenting the Child You Have,* the book)

1. **Patience**—Allow yourself to take the time you need to make decisions.

2. **Time alone**—Time away from your kids and family to remember who you are and clear your energy is vital.
3. **Sampling others' energy**—Feel and sample the energy of your kids and others, but don't take it on as your own.
4. **Waiting for a lunar cycle**—You don't need to be rushed into other people's time frames for things. It's okay to slow things down that require your presence and effort. Share parenting duties in a way that meets everyone's needs. Don't get stuck in gender roles and duties.
5. **Listen to how you feel**—Because you are sensitive to your environment, if places or people don't feel good to you, trust your knowing and change the circumstances. If it's a big decision, such as moving or changing relationship dynamics, remember to give it at least a lunar cycle to contemplate it.

Journal Prompts for Reflector Parents

First, we will explore your *childhood* experience as a Reflector

1. Did you feel different from your family and friends?
2. Did your family interact with you in a way that supported your unique needs?
3. How do you feel they could have supported you better?
4. What do you wish you would have received from your parents/family/friends growing up?
5. When did you know you were different from most of the people around you? What was your experience of those differences?
6. What is something that would have made you feel more seen as a child?

Next, we will explore your *adulthood* as a Reflector

1. How do you feel about your worthiness of love, affection, and connection?
2. How have you changed and adapted throughout your life?
3. What have you learned about yourself and others from your experiences with other people?
4. What feelings or sensations do you have in your body when your environment is not correct for you?
5. Do you rush your decisions or give yourself plenty of time? What is that like?
6. Can you think of a time when you took your time with a decision, and it paid off? Write about that experience.
7. How has understanding your Human Design affected your decision-making and understanding of yourself?

In this last set of questions, we will explore your *parenting* as a Reflector

1. How are your kids similar to or different from you?
2. If you have kids with a lot of energy or quick inner Authorities (such as Sacral or Splenic), how do you navigate honoring their decision-making process without compromising yours?
3. How do you experience your identity as a Reflector parent?
4. What grace do you allow yourself to have time alone each day?
5. What words do you hear pop out of your mouth and sound like a parent figure you grew up with that leave you a little stunned? How does that make you feel toward yourself and your child?

These questions are for parents of any energy type with a Reflector energy type child. So, if you are a Manifestor, Manifesting Generator, Generator, Projector, or Reflector, and you have a Reflector child, this section is for you.

REFLECTOR CHILD

What Parents Need to Learn about Their Reflector Children

1. **Rarity**—Your child's energy type represents less than one percent of the population. You'll need to approach parenting them differently.
2. **They need time**—Decisions can take at least one lunar cycle for them. Bigger decisions can take multiple lunar cycles.
3. **They reflect others' energy and emotions**—Look at yourself or the people around your child when their behavior seems unusual for them. How are you or others behaving? Do they feel good with the people they are around or the place they are in? If not, it will reflect in their behavior and emotions.
4. **Time alone**—They need time and space to themselves to understand their own energy.
5. **Your energy feels stabilizing to them**—Until age seven, children's auras aren't fully developed and stabilized, so when they are in an uncomfortable place or with people that they aren't sure of, they will cling to you more. Your aura is familiar and comforting.
6. **Chameleons**—They reflect the people and environment around them. As they change friend groups, they will adapt to the people around them, and you'll see their interests change.

What a Reflector Child Needs and Needs to Learn

1. **They're adaptable**—They are open to experiencing life through other people and will reflect that. They are not copying them but mirroring them through their nature to experience the many ways people are in the world and to gain wisdom about humanity.
2. **They need time and patience**—They can and need to take their time (a lunar cycle—twenty-nine days) to make a big decision.

3. **Alone time**—They need plenty of alone time to get out of other people's auras and connect with their true selves.

4. **Sounding boards**—They will need to verbally process their thoughts and feelings with a trusted person who will hold space for them and not tell them what to do or how to feel.

Journal Prompts for a Parent with a Reflector Child

1. How do you notice your Reflector child mirroring you or other family members/friends?

2. Does your Reflector child have ample opportunities to experience many different auras? I.e., school, playgroups, clubs, activities, etc.

3. How do you allow your child space to take their time with big (for them) decisions?

4. What is one area that you feel you need to lean into and grow more around in raising a Reflector child?

5. What was the biggest *aha!* you learned about your child being a Reflector energy type?

6. What has been the most exciting thing to watch and learn as your child has grown so far?

7. How do you notice that different environments affect your child?

CHAPTER FOUR

AUTHORITY

Mind is Not Your Authority

Our brains are wonderful complex organs that help us process information, warn us of potential threats to safety, and regulate systems in our bodies like temperature, hormones, heartbeat, and more. They sustain life. But when it comes to the mind—the mental process of the brain—we tend to rely on it to make decisions and often end up feeling very stressed. The problem with this is that we have all lived in a conditioning field where we take in information from everyone around us. Most of our conditioning comes from our childhood, especially those first seven years of life. Conditioning affects how we make decisions leading us to decide with our minds rather than our body's innate wisdom by first considering how someone else would respond to our decision or how our decision might affect others rather than what we truly want. Part of the fault in this way of thinking is that we can never know how someone else will respond to what we do or say. We may anticipate a pattern repeating with the person in how they respond but, ultimately, they can choose to respond however they like. That is not our responsibility. This is not to say that we shouldn't consider others in our decisions, but that we must first be clear on what we genuinely want so we don't live our lives trying to make others happy while ignoring our own needs and desires.

We do have a responsibility to communicate our decisions, needs, and thoughts in a kind way, but we can never know how someone else will respond. Even if you say the nicest thing in the world to someone, showering them with praise, they may think that you are making fun of them or lying to them because of their own lived experiences as they project onto you. We cannot stop them from thinking what they think, which is why when we make decisions out of our conditioned minds, we make decisions that often don't support ourselves *or* the other person. No one's needs are really being met because you've made a decision that you *think* should be right.

However, when we are able to connect with our inner Authority, which comes from our innate intelligence and body's wisdom, and trust it, we can use it to make aligned decisions for ourselves, which in turn allows others to tap into their inner Authority and make decisions that support them and their needs. This is honest. Being honest is not always easy, but it's true.

We live in a world where people don't want to rock the boat, so to speak, and will go along with what they think others want from them, leading them to live a life that does not feel authentic. It takes so much energy to live this way! We waste so much time not speaking our truths and trying to be what others want us to be.

Imagine what it would be like to have a choice pop up in your life, a decision to be made, and not have to rely on your mind to process it. Making a decision that you feel aligned with, rather than getting lost in what others will think is your path to freedom, more time, and better boundaries. It doesn't come all at once but is learned over time as you begin to play with this way of decision-making and incorporate it into your life. Begin with the more minor things in life and work your way up to the bigger stuff as you gain confidence in trusting your inner Authority.

Trusting your inner Authority requires you to take a step back from trying to control all the outcomes in your life and realize that when you surrender to the process, life will unfold as it is meant to. Not all results will feel great. Sometimes choosing what is right for you is difficult for someone else, but your truth will set you free. And your truth will allow the other person to have their own experience of that decision that is based on their truth. Life is not meant to be easy, uncomplicated, or to feel good all the time. It is often through the difficult things that we grow the most and learn who we truly are.

To find your inner Authority, please reference your chart. You'll see it listed as either "inner Authority" or simply, "Authority" in the chart details.

As you go through these journal prompts, first explore your inner Authority, and then use the journal questions to explore the inner Authority of your children, partner, or parents, as you explore the parent-child relationships in your life.

Emotional Authority

Note—If you are a Generator or Manifesting Generator, also see the Sacral Authority as it is part of how you make decisions while you wait for emotional clarity.

The Emotional Authority represents about fifty percent of the population and is found in any person with a defined Emotional Solar Plexus in their chart. Having an Emotional Authority means that you will move through one or several emotional wave types throughout your days and need to give yourself time to make decisions, especially big decisions. Making choices in the highs or lows of your emotional wave can lead to regret or disappointment later on if you pass up an opportunity when you were in a low or agreed to something you later regretted when in an emotional high. Remember to at least sleep on bigger decisions and don't be afraid to ask for more time. If the opportunity is right for you, it will still be there when you reach clarity.

Journal Prompts for Emotional Authority

1. Do you feel confident in making decisions based on how you feel?
   a. If so, describe how you know when you're making an aligned decision through emotional clarity. What does it feel like in your body?
   b. If not, let's explore where that may come from. Let's take a trip back to your childhood. Can you recall a time when you were so excited and passionate about something, and your parents made you wait to make the commitment? This may have been something small like going to a friend's birthday party or something bigger like taking a photography class. When you knew this was a yes for you, and you had to wait it out, how did it feel? Did your excitement remain high even when you had to wait? Did you feel a particular feeling in your body that told you it was a definite yes for you?
   c. Now let's contrast that with a time when you had to wait, but your *yes* turned into a *no*. What was something you were so set on having or doing as a kid, and you had to wait, and then your feelings on the matter changed by the time your parents said you could have or do that thing? What did that feel like in your body?

   d. Can you feel a difference in your body even now when you reflect on those two instances?

2. Think back to a time when you made a decision that turned out to be so aligned and right that you had a great experience. What was one of the best decisions you ever made?

   a. What made it a great decision?

   b. How did you know it was correct for you?

   c. Were there any sensations in your body that told you it was aligned for you? If so, what were they?

   d. Emotional clarity is never 100 percent certain. What do you need to feel confident when waiting and making a decision? Do you trust that you need more time to make decisions for bigger things? What's the longest it's taken for you to make a big decision?

3. Do you trust yourself to make good decisions? If so, describe what your self-trust feels like.

4. *This prompt may bring up triggering memories. Please skip if it's too fresh or painful until you have professional support to process what may come up.* If you don't feel like you can trust yourself to make good decisions, where or when did you learn you could not be trusted to make good decisions for yourself?

5. For some people with Emotional Authority, their *no* can feel like a rock in their stomach or a dropping sensation or an emptiness in their body. You may or may not identify with these feelings but see if you can tap into what your *no* feels like in your body. Where do you feel it, and what sensations does it give you? Alternatively, some people describe the *yes* for Emotional Authority as a lightness, joy, or rise in energy.

This inner Authority is truly about how you feel, and you can only know how you feel about something when you've given it enough time to feel your way through your emotional wave(s).

1. What waves do you have defined in your chart? Collective? Individual? Tribal?
    a. **Tribal waves (Channels 19-49, 37-40, 59-6)**—What do you notice about your wave? Do you know what things ratchet you up in your wave faster? I find there are often needs, desires, or boundaries that are not met when this wave ratchets higher, especially things such as fatigue (non-Sacrals and hermits—line 2's) or feeling the pressure of others (open Root Center or Head Center). These are just a couple of examples of how this might present.
    b. **Individual waves (Channels 39-55, 22-12)**—What do you need to help yourself *not* make decisions in the highs or lows of your wave when everything feels more intense? How can you remind yourself to not pass up an opportunity when in the low of a wave, or say yes in the high of a wave that you might later regret?
    c. **Collective waves (Channels 41-30, 36-35)**—Do you allow yourself to enter into things without high expectations, or do you deeply attach to the outcome? How can you hold your vision and excitement while surrendering to the process?
2. How aware are you of how often you feel the highs or lows of your wave?
3. What happens when you make decisions in the high of your wave?
4. What happens when you make decisions in the low of your wave?
5. Describe a time when you were in the high of your wave, and you made a commitment that you later regretted and wanted out of. What did that feel like through the process? What did you do?

6. Describe a time when you were in the low of your wave, and you passed up an opportunity you later regretted. What did that feel like through the process? What did you do?
7. What do you need when you're in the low of your wave (rest, boundaries, time alone, nature, etc.)? In the high of your wave (someone to help be the voice of reason, reminder to wait a little longer, etc.)?
8. What does the middle of your wave feel like to you?
9. What signs do you have that tell you that you need more time to make a decision?
10. What things in life do you need to take more time to make decisions about?

Exercise for Using Your Emotional Authority

Please reference chapter seven in *Parenting the Child You Have*, the book, for more details on how the emotional waves operate.

To connect with this inner Authority, it's important to understand your emotional wave(s). What pattern are they? How often do they rise and fall? What do you need in the highs to not jump into a decision you might regret? And what do you need to not pass up an opportunity in the lows that you might regret? Who can help you wait out your waves?

1. Grab a calendar, or use the one on your phone.
2. Using a scale from -10 to +10, each day rate where you feel you are in your wave. If you have a wave that moves quickly, make a note of this several times a day.
3. When you feel high or low in your wave, also note what that feels like. What emotions or physical sensations do you feel?
4. And just as important, make note of how you feel in the middle of your wave. This can often feel like an absence of feeling, especially if you have a wave with big extremes such as the Individual wave, but it is important to understand. This is the place you want to make a decision from after you traveled the ups

and downs of your wave, so get familiar with what it feels like. Is there a sensation in your body when you feel confident to make a good decision for yourself?

5. When you make decisions that have a bigger impact on your life, make note of how you felt when making that decision. Over time you may notice you have a specific feeling in your body or an inner alignment that you feel when the decision is right.
6. Be gentle with yourself. An Emotional Authority is never 100 percent certain, so learn to find the place where it feels correct for you to say yes or no.

Sacral Authority

The Sacral Authority is exclusive to Generators and Manifesting Generators, who are the only energy types with a defined Sacral Center. This Sacral Center definition gives them a consistent workforce and life force energy. It is the Authority for Generators and Manifesting Generators when the Emotional Solar Plexus (ESP) is *not* defined in the chart. The Sacral Center is also important even when the ESP is the Authority because it is the Generator's and Manifesting Generator's inner compass helping them to know what is true and correct for them in the moment. It bypasses the mind's conditioning to get to the truth of the matter when it has not been conditioned out of them.

The Sacral Authority belongs to Generators or Manifesting Generators only, who represent about 70 percent of the population. Not all Generators or Manifesting Generators will have a Sacral Authority; however, all will have access to this wisdom. A Generator or Manifesting Generator may have either Sacral or Emotional Authority.

Journal Prompts for Sacral Authority

1. Would you like to explore this Authority and how it feels in your body right now? If so, continue on. If not, skip and come back to these questions when your Sacral says yes.
2. Did your gut response or knowing ever keep you safe from harm? How did you know to trust it? What did it feel or sound like?
3. What does it feel like when your Sacral says yes or no?
4. Do you feel your yes/no in your belly? Lower? Higher? Do you feel a sensation of a physical pulling toward or pushing away? Do you feel a surge of energy when it's a yes? Do you nod or shake your head? What sounds do you make that tell you yes or no? I.e., yes, no, uh-huh/unh-uh, yep, nope.
5. Think back to one really great decision you made. If you can, think back to making the decision and what it felt like in your body and describe it. How did you know it was right and aligned for you?
6. Do you feel confused when people ask you open-ended questions such as "Where would you like to go for dinner?" rather than closed, yes/no questions such as "Would you like to go get tacos tonight?" How do you let others know you need yes/no, this/that types of questions to be able to respond without getting frustrated?
7. When making decisions, do you go to a mind-oriented practice such as a pro/con list, or do you allow your gut (Sacral) to guide you?
8. What do you do when your mind says yes, and your Sacral says no? Or when the mind says no, and your Sacral says yes?
9. What would allow you to lean in more and begin to trust your Sacral more often?
10. Would you like to write about a time you trusted your gut?
11. Would you like to write about a time you didn't trust your gut?

Exercise for Using Your Sacral Authority

1. Write down all of the things you're trying to decide about on three-by-five cards.
2. Have someone else shuffle them with cards that ask you simple and easy questions, such as "Are you sitting down?" "Do you like bananas?" "Is it raining?" etc.
3. Next, find a partner to read through the cards, quickly tossing them into yes or no piles. The only rules are that you have up to two seconds to answer, and you can only say yes or no. There are no maybes and no hesitation. If you hesitate or think *maybe,* it's a no.
4. In the end, pick up all of your yes cards and see what your Sacral energy truly is available for and what you want to use it on.
5. Next, look through your noes and see what surprises you.
   a. If you have Emotional Authority, then repeat this daily or weekly until you have moved through the highs and lows of your wave and reached clarity.
   b. If your answer consistently stays a yes, it's a yes.
   c. If you get some yes and some no, consider it a no for now.
   d. You can keep checking on your answer but consider if you are checking because your mind is unwilling to let it go or if you need something more to be able to move forward with a yes.

A second step you can take is to take your pile of noes and ask secondary questions such as:

   e. Do I want to quit this?
   f. Am I ready to let this go?
   g. Do I need more resources (time, energy, support, information, etc.) to continue?
   h. Am I just frustrated this is not going as quickly as I want it to?

Another way to do this on your own is to write down the choices you're deciding upon on sticky notes and each day go through them quickly putting them in yes/no piles and then notice what you chose. If you also have an Emotional Authority, repeat this daily or weekly and keep a journal or photo of your responses to track them over time to get clarity.

Splenic Authority

Splenic Authority is an inner Authority for Manifestors or Projectors. Splenic energy is related to survival, instinct, intuition, timing, and the immune system. This type of knowing is instinctual and in the moment, therefore ***it does not repeat***, as it is constantly scanning the horizon and alerting you to potential threats. This is why it is more common to feel or hear a no with this inner Authority than it is to feel or hear a yes. It is often the absence of the no that signals things are okay. The caveat is that you must be connected and alert to the signals coming from this highly intuitive center to hear its warning.

This Authority starkly contrasts Emotional Authority, which needs time for clarity, while Splenic Authority is the opposite and provides instant in-the-moment knowing. Children with this Authority can make quick decisions easily and be sure of what they want in the moment. The only caveat with this is that, because the Spleen is about safety and security and is constantly scanning for new information, it can change quickly. If it senses new information that feels as if it might compromise its safety, the decision can change. The Splenic knowing is a whisper telling them to trust or not, to go or not, whether it's healthy or not, and is based on whether it feels safe and correct. It's more of a whisper that says "Stop" or "Don't" rather than "Yes!"

The Splenic Authority's in-the-moment knowing does not repeat, so asking repeatedly for an answer does not help your child get clearer and can lead them to distrust their Authority. As a parent, it may be confusing because their answer seems to change depending on when you ask them, but remember, they are constantly taking in new information to base their decision upon.

When I think of this Authority, I think of big cats or other wild animals that use their senses to know if it's safe or not. The saying "it made the hairs on the back of my neck stand up" would be appropriate to convey the subtlety of this inner knowing.

Journal Prompts for Splenic Authority

1. Do you trust your Splenic knowing? How do you know you can trust it?
2. With your Splenic knowing, do you hear, feel, sense, smell, see, or have another way of connecting to your intuition and knowing?
3. How does your way of knowing guide you to the right decisions for you?
4. Do you notice your noes are louder than your yeses? Or the opposite? What is that like for you?
5. Where in your body do you feel your yes or no?
6. Write about a time when you listened to your no, and it was helpful.
7. What other senses might be involved in your knowing?
8. Have you always been someone who could sense things that others didn't notice? If so, how did that benefit you?

Exercise for Using Your Splenic Authority

This inner Authority is about perception, sensing, and feeling. The biggest challenge is to trust what you know in the moment and to not second guess yourself.

Because this Authority is so connected to intuition, you need to be able to connect with it easily to rely on it for making decisions. If you struggle making decisions with this Authority, you may just need to spend some more time by yourself when making decisions. Connect with nature, or try forest bathing, meditating, or any other practice that helps you to get in touch with your body and senses, and ground into your sense of self.

Remember, you don't need more time to make decisions like those with Emotional or Sacral Authorities. Your decisions are made in the moment when you connect to your truth and don't allow your mind to take over.

It may be helpful to have a physical representation of your choices in front of you and then see which one you're most drawn to. Does your body lean in toward one immediately? Do you feel repelled away from one or more of the choices?

Start with choices of small consequences such as which food to have for dinner or what to do on your fifteen-minute break. After you've made the decision, and proceed with your choice, reflect upon the experience and recall what you felt in the moment that guided you to the choice you made. If this choice felt aligned, make note of the sensations that guided you to the correct choice. Also make note of the sensations that told you this was not the best choice for you. Often, in the beginning we have to look at our behaviors and choices in hindsight to begin to understand what works and what doesn't. Go easy on yourself and consider it all an experiment. What happens if you try?

For children with this Authority, help them learn to trust their inner Authority by not second-guessing them. Let them decide based on what they know to be true in that moment. If circumstances change, be willing to change directions with them.

Ego Authority

This inner Authority may be found in charts of a Manifestor or Projector. An Ego Manifested Authority will be found in a Manifestor, while an Ego Projected Authority will be found in a Projector.

The Ego-Manifested Authority

A Manifestor can manifest what they are called to create or do without support from anyone else and can act on their inspirations. The Ego Manifested Authority can feel very powerful and even seem somewhat egotistical to others as it comes from the Will Center, which is also known as the Ego Center. It comes from a place of "I want this," "I want to do that," and is very "I" driven. The Will Center is related to the energy of "What do I want?" and "Do I have the resources to take this on?" Even though the voice can sound like me, me, me, the Will Center correlates with the heart chakra and has a tribal element to it, based on the tribal circuitry that runs through it. The motivations behind "I want" and "I need" are bigger than the individual "I" in its purest form.

The Manifestor is designed to significantly impact others, so when it speaks from the Ego Authority, it can feel powerful and lead the Manifestor to become conditioned to filter what they say so others receive it better. This conditioning quiets the Authority of the Ego Manifestor as they try to make themselves small, to want for nothing, and to people-please instead because that seems to make everyone happier.

The challenge is for them to stand in their Authority and power by continuing to say those "I" statements and to make sure they're informing those who will be impacted by what they intend to do. So perhaps rather than "I need a car," which can leave those around them wondering if they are asking for money for a car, try adding in the element of informing, such as "I need a car. I'm going to get a job and save money so I can drive myself to school."

Journal Prompts for Ego Manifested Authority

1. Do you allow yourself to use statements that begin with "I want" or "I need"?
2. What are your perceptions of the way you have made decisions or informed others of what you wanted or needed?
3. How do you see yourself based on others' reactions to your "I want/I need" statements?
4. How might you see your words or actions differently now through the lens of your Human Design inner Authority?
5. What do you need to feel comfortable trusting your inner Authority?
6. How can you honor your inner Authority, while still being kind and compassionate to others?
7. How concerned are you with the perceptions of other family, friends, peers, etc.?
8. What could you do to support yourself with this inner Authority to remain connected to your innate knowing?
9. What does a yes feel like in your body? What sensations might it have?

The Ego-Projected Inner Authority

The Ego-Projected Authority belongs to the Projector. It is a rare Authority as it only occurs in Projectors that have the Will Center and the G Center defined through Channel 25-51. Projectors must wait to be recognized and for the correct invitation. Ego Projected Projectors respond to the invitation from a place of "I do (or do not) have the energy/resources for that." They need to be selfish and ask themselves the questions, "What's in it for me? What do I want?" in response to the invitations they receive. Waiting for invitations can feel like they take forever to arrive for the Projector. While waiting, it's important that they refine their craft, learn a system, and become a resource for something in order to receive the invitations that are right for them, to be recognized, and to respond. While waiting for correct invitations, it's important with all the open centers in their chart that they don't act from the conditioned mind, jumping into things they do not have the energy for or have not been invited into. You can help your child understand this Authority by asking them questions such as "How do you think it will be beneficial to you if you say yes or no?" or "What opportunity will you be passing up if you say no?" or even "Why do you want it?"

Journal Prompts for Ego Projected Authority

1. How many times in your life have you been told that it's "not all about you"?
2. Have you been conditioned (through others' responses to you) that you should not think of yourself first when making decisions?
3. What comes up for you when you think about responding with what you want in response to an offer or opportunity?
4. How often do you respond with "I want" or "I don't want" rather than "Well..."? The true response of the Ego Authority has a voice of "I," but society can condition people with an Ego Authority to not speak from "I," which leads them back to their minds to make decisions that are not correct for them.
5. When you make a decision, do you consider whether you have the resources to say yes? If so, what resources do you take into consideration? I.e., time, energy, money, etc.
6. How much do you consider how others will be affected by your saying yes or no?

Exercise for Using Your Ego Authority

This inner Authority can get called out for being too selfish, but really, it truly is about whether you want to commit to this choice or not. If you do not want to do something and say yes, you won't be happy, will struggle, or things will fall apart.

Spend some time alone getting in touch with what makes you feel aligned. Take a trip by yourself and decide every step of the way what you want to do. Without another person there, you're free to say yes to yourself and your Ego Authority. If you can't get away for a trip alone, try taking yourself out to lunch or spend the day in your town exploring only what you want to and not doing any chores or tasks. Make the day or a few hours only about you.

At the end of your alone journey, spend some time journaling about your experience. What did you do for yourself that you would have said no to otherwise because of what you thought others would say about your choice? What did it feel like to not consider everyone else's needs, wants, desires, and opinions? Did you notice a feeling in your body when you were making decisions that felt great? Did you notice a feeling in your body when you felt like you were supposed to make a decision other than what you wanted? How could you use those feelings to guide you in knowing when a decision is aligned for you?

If your child has this inner Authority, let them have an adventure day where you say yes to their "I want" and "I need" as often as possible and honor their nos. Pay attention to how they respond when you meet their yeses and noes. What do you notice about their confidence and connection to what they say yes or no to?

Self Authority

The Self Authority is only found in Projectors. This inner Authority is concerned with making decisions that feel aligned with the truth of who they are at their core. With their defined G Center, they are here to know who they are and the direction they are taking in life, even if that direction changes over time. When they make a decision, they respond by running the decision through a filter of "Does this feel aligned with the direction of my life?" And "Does this make me feel more or less like myself?" "Do I feel seen and recognized for being me?"

Journal Prompts for Self Authority

1. What does the definition in your G Center tell you about what consistent energy is present for you in your Identity (G) Center? Look at the theme of the defined gates and channels here to learn more.
2. What makes you feel most like you? What makes you feel seen?
3. Ask yourself, "Does this feel like the right direction for me?"
4. What does it feel like to be recognized for who you are? What things are you being called out for?
5. When you make a decision for yourself, do you consider if saying yes makes you feel more aligned with the truth of who you are and the direction you're going?
    a. If yes, explain your current direction and how you determine if it aligns.
    b. If no, what would it feel like if you did run your decisions through this filter?

Spend time alone to connect with your identity and direction and what makes you feel like you when making your decisions.

Exercise for Using Your Self Projected Authority

Projector, what makes you feel seen for who you truly are? Anchoring into this truth is the key to aligning with your inner authority.

Spend some time reflecting on who you are, what you stand for, and what is important to you. What direction are you moving toward in your life? Are you in alignment with this direction? If not, what helps you reconnect with your true north?

Start a journal of decision-making experiments. When you make a decision that you're sure about, write down what made you feel it was right for you. What did it feel like in your body? In your soul? Within your being?

When you make a decision that turns out not to be correct for you, reflect and write down the red flags for what made you realize it wasn't right for you. Were you compromising what you wanted for someone else? Compromising is not a bad thing, but first, being clear on what you want allows you to go into negotiations with clear boundaries of how far you will bend. If it takes you away from feeling like yourself and compromising who you are, it's likely not right for you. Write down your experiences and notice what your telling signs are. Do you feel it in your body? Does something click within your being? Do you notice a feeling of resistance?

Mental Authority/Environmental Authority/No Authority

Mental Authority, also known as Environmental Authority or No Authority, is found only in Projectors. With so much openness in their chart, combined with a lot of activity in the mind, it is so very important to allow yourself to have the space to process your thoughts out loud where you can hear yourself and what filters through you based on your environment.

It is critical that you are in an environment that feels good to you when you make your decisions. If you are in an uncomfortable place or the people around you don't feel good energetically to be around, you may struggle to make a decision or may make a decision you later regret.

Though you need people (sounding boards) to bounce your thoughts off of and, ideally, who help reflect back to you what they hear from you, you do not need advice on what to do. You need good questions that allow you to contemplate your inner world. Though there can be a lot of external processing, in the end you'll feel something within you when you have reached the correct decision for yourself. You should feel free to take the time you need to reach your decision and not be rushed.

Journal Prompts for Mental Authority/Environmental Authority/ No Authority

Questions you may ask yourself are:

1. How am I feeling about making this decision?
2. Am I in a place or with people who feel good to me while making my decision?
3. Who would be a good person to talk to about my decision, a person who won't advise me but will help me gain clarity?
4. What do I need to be able to make a decision?
5. Do I feel that saying yes will put me into an environment that feels good, with people that feel good?

Exercise for Using Your Mental Authority

Questions to journal about for clarity on understanding how your inner Authority makes decisions:

1. How aware are you of your environment and how it makes you feel?
2. What happens when you feel pushed into making a decision when you don't feel like things are right around you such as the people you're with or place you're in?
3. How were you taught to make decisions as a child?
4. What inner Authorities did your parents/caregivers have (if known)? How did their ways of making decisions affect how you make decisions now?
5. How do you give yourself time to make a decision?
6. Is there a feeling in your body that tells you when a decision is in alignment for you? If so, what is it?

Lunar Authority

The Lunar Authority is exclusive to the Reflector. This inner Authority needs a full lunar cycle (twenty-nine) to make aligned decisions for themselves. During this lunar cycle, the moon transits all sixty-four gates in the Human Design system, allowing the Reflector to experience definition in each of the gates through the transits. During this time, they need people to be their sounding boards, so they can process their decision. They do not need advice during this time, but someone to talk with who might bring aspects of their decision to light that they may not see on their own. The worst thing for this inner Authority is to feel rushed or pressured into a decision. Learn to lean into the trust that if the opportunity is correct, it will still be there for you if it's aligned. Bigger decisions may need several lunar cycles to make a decision while simple everyday decisions, such as what to have for dinner or what to do that day, do not need as much time, generally speaking. No need to meal-plan a month out. However, before moving to a new city, for example, they need time to really consider this decision. Additionally, sometimes Reflectors have contemplated a big decision for a while before they bring it to others and may be farther along in their decision-making process and can make a decision in what appears to be less than a full lunar cycle.

Journal Prompts for Lunar Authority

1. How in tune with the energies of the moon are you?
2. When in the moon cycle, do you feel your best? Around the new moon? Full moon? Somewhere in between?
3. When in your life have you waited for an entire lunar cycle to make a decision and it turned out great? What was great about it? How did you know it was the right decision for you?
4. When in your life have you not waited for an entire lunar cycle to make a decision and it didn't turn out well? Describe how that went and what you learned from it.
5. Who are the trusted sounding boards that allow you to talk out your decisions without advising you on what you should do? Do you have different people for different areas of life decisions?

6. If you could go back in time and give your ten-year-old self advice on how to make aligned decisions, what would you say, and how could that have changed your life?
7. How do you know, after waiting for a lunar cycle, that a decision is a yes for you? Do you feel something internally? If so, what does it feel like?

Exercise for Using Your Lunar Authority

Learn about the gates of the Human Design system as the moon transits them each day. You can go to any popular Human Design software or app and see the transits as they shift each day.

The moon goes through two to three gates each day, which means that in a month, you will experience the energy of all sixty-four gates. Getting to know each of these energies will help you to align with when it feels best to make decisions about different things in your life.

As you intentionally tune into each of these gates, keep a journal of how you feel and what you notice about the emotions, reactions, fears, and people around you.

Inner Authority Self Reflection (All Inner Authorities)

- Do you believe you know what is best for yourself and your family? If so, why? If not, why? Is there someone else you trust more to make the decisions for you or your family, and why?
- What is your inner Authority? What are the inner Authorities of the family members closest to you or the people you live with or interact most often with?
- Think of a time in your life when you made a great decision for yourself and spend some time reflecting on how you made that decision. Was it aligned with what you know about your inner Authority now? Did you know instantly it was right for you, or did it take some time? How did the way you made this great decision in your life align with your inner Authority?

Child(ren)/Family Inner Authority Reflection

If you don't feel confident in your own inner Authority yet, I recommend you skip this section until you've completed the rest of the workbook, and then return to this section with your child/family members' charts to complete.

1. How does this child/person make decisions? What is their inner Authority?
2. How does your inner Authority compare with theirs? Do you both have faster or slower inner authorities or does one of you have a quick and one a slower Authority? How does that affect your relationship in decision-making?
3. Do you override their inner Authority with your decision-making, or try to get them to make decisions in the same way as you? Do they push you into making a decision faster than you are comfortable with?
4. How many different inner Authorities do you have in your home? Who has the same inner Authority? What do you notice about how aligned each person is with their inner Authority?
5. What are your parents' inner Authorities? Did they make decisions aligned with their inner Authority, or were they conditioned to make decisions from their minds?
6. How did your family's alignment with their inner Authority affect your ability to make decisions using your inner Authority growing up? Were you taught to make decisions the way they did? Or did they allow you to honor your process?
7. What do you want to teach your children about their inner Authority?

CHAPTER FIVE

EMOTIONS

When we view emotions through the lens of Human Design, it allows us to get some distance from what we feel and learn to discern how we feel and experience emotions. We also learn that we are not our emotions. Everyone *feels* emotions. People with a defined Emotional Solar Plexus Center (ESP) are constantly moving through their emotional waves and feelings, while those with an undefined Emotional Center are feeling in response to a stimulus.

Learning to discern what you feel within yourself versus what you feel from the environment around you can help you change or deepen your relationship with your emotions and those of the people around you.

Noticing the emotional patterns of your children, family, and people you spend the most time with, in addition to your own patterns, can create a life that is filled with more connection, creativity, passion, better boundaries, and a deeper understanding of the human condition.

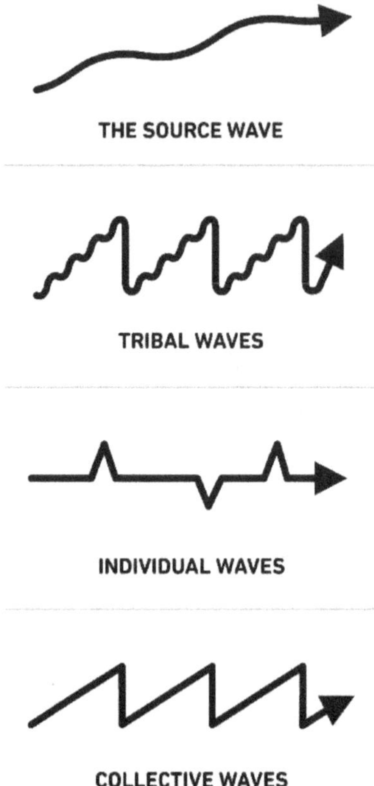

Defined Emotional Solar Plexus

1. If you have a defined ESP, which channel(s) do you have?
    a. Tribal waves—Channels 19-49, 37-40, 59-6
    b. Individual waves—Channels 39-55, 22-12
    c. Collective waves—Channels 41-30, 36-35
2. Do you consider yourself an emotional person? Write about why or why not.
3. Do other people tell you that your emotions are intense or avoid you when you express strong emotions? If so, how does that make you feel?
4. Do you notice how your emotions affect those around you with undefined ESPs?

5. What patterns do you notice about how long your wave takes to rise and fall? What does it feel like?
6. Do you try to minimize your emotions to not affect others/avoid conflict?
7. Do you have a child with an undefined ESP? If so, how do you handle their tantrums/meltdowns? How would you like it to be different?
8. What do you notice about your child with a defined ESP and how they relate to their emotions? How would you like it to be different? What would you like them to learn about their emotions?
9. What do you need when your wave rises? What do you need when it falls?
   a. **Tribal waves—Channels 19-49, 37-40, 59-6**

      These waves usually have an unmet need that makes them ratchet higher until they either explode or reach clarity. They often respond well to touch to bring them back down.

      i. Do you know what needs are not being met when your wave explodes?
      ii. What do you notice helps you to reset?
      iii. Do you find that those around you feel okay when you have an explosion?
      iv. If not, how do you pick up the pieces and move forward?
      v. How do you make amends?
      vi. How do you own your responsibility around your emotional reactions with your kids or family?

   b. **Individual waves—Channels 39-55, 22-12**

      These waves usually spend most of their time in a more neutral state but have sudden highs and lows that can feel unexpected.

      i. What do you need when you're in the low of your wave?
      ii. Does expressing your emotions through art, music, or movement help you release or process your feelings?

iii. What do you want others to know about you and your emotional wave and what you need?

c. **Collective waves—Channels 41-30, 36-35**

These waves build on expectation and rise higher and higher until an expectation is not met, and they come crashing down where they can remain until a new wave begins building again.

i. How often do you find yourself imagining how decisions will turn out?

ii. Do you get attached to the outcome before things have even begun?

iii. How often do you find yourself disappointed with outcomes or with other people?

iv. What would it look like to release the outcome and enter into things just for the experience of it?

Exercises for Children with Defined Emotional Centers

These kids have one, two, or all three types of emotional waves that they move through at all times, based on their chart definition. You can help them understand what these waves feel like by tracking their emotions with the emotions chart on a calendar. You can also help them by encouraging them to connect to what they need when they are in the highs or lows of their waves.

If you see your child with a tribal wave ratcheting up to an explosion, use touch, like an offer of a hug or a gentle hand on the shoulder to help them regulate, and ask them what they need. This wave operates through needs so helping them to identify and ask for what they need can help lessen the number of emotional explosions they experience.

If your child has an individual wave, when they are in the lows, ask them what they need. Do they need space to be alone? Do they need to have a chill day or afternoon and not have to fulfill all the typical obligations? Where can you help them learn to recognize what they need and find ways to give that to themselves? When they are in the highs of their waves, help them recognize that though they might want to jump into things, they need to give themselves time to feel through their wave and see if they still want to say yes to whatever is exciting to them in the high of the wave.

If your child has a Collective wave, practice using phrases such as "We're not sure how things will turn out, but it's about the journey rather than the destination," "We don't know what we'll find when we get to the destination, but let's look at it as an adventure." "Adventures are about not knowing how things will turn out and finding a way to embrace and accept that. What is one thing you like about what we're doing/what's happening right now?" Ask them these questions on the journey to help them stay present and not live in the future expecting a certain outcome; that way their waves don't have to crash down into the lows so often.

And remember, language matters. Using phrases such as "*I feel* sad/happy/angry/frustrated/bitter/excited" rather than "*I am* sad/happy/angry/frustrated/bitter/excited" can make a big difference in how they view themselves and how they relate to the emotions that they feel.

Undefined Emotional Solar Plexus

1. If you have an open ESP, how do you take in the emotions of those around you?
2. Who in your family has a defined ESP?
   a. Do you avoid them or feel comfortable with their emotions?
3. Do you have a child with a defined ESP? If so, how do you handle their tantrums/meltdowns? How would you like it to be different?
4. Do your strong emotional reactions bother you? Those of others?
5. What have you learned about the people you're closest to who have an emotional wave?
6. How has learning about the emotional waves shifted your relationship with emotions?

7. How has learning about the emotional waves shifted your relationship with emotions?
8. Do you have a child with an undefined ESP? How do you experience their emotions? How does your child experience and relate to the emotions they feel?
9. How do you help your child learn to identify the emotions they feel without connecting them to their identity? I.e., using language such as "I feel" rather than "I am."
10. What do the emotional waves of the people in your home or closest to you feel like? How do you respond to them?
11. How do you navigate the emotional dynamic in the workplace or community spaces?

Exercises for Children with Undefined Emotional Centers

For younger children, you can use the emotional faces below to help them identify the feelings they have before they can describe them with words.

As children begin spending all day in a classroom, they pick up the emotional environment around them at school not knowing that they are not the source of the emotions and bring them home with them. To help them leave it at the door and not believe these emotions are theirs, they can illustrate three-by-five cards with faces on them that show emotions. Encourage them to draw what the feelings feel like to them. This may be a face, a person, or it may be an abstract representation of what they feel. Anger, for example, might be scribbles that feel chaotic, and they press down hard with their pen to draw. Whatever it feels like to them is what should be represented, not your idea of what that emotion feels or looks like. Place these on a table or area near your door. When they come home from school, ask them if they feel any of these emotions. Ask them to take the cards that represent the emotions they are feeling and put them in a designated bowl by the door to represent letting them go—they aren't theirs. Alternatively, you can tie a string to them and have them hang them up on a coat rack just like they would their coat or backpack when they come in to represent leaving those feelings at the door.

You can take this a step further and ask them if they feel like any of those emotions are theirs and what they relate to. If they can tell you, you can help them process those emotions together. This is an opportunity to help them notice if moving their body through exercise, dance, singing, or another physical release would make them feel better. They may just need some quiet time to process or release the emotional energy as well. Ask them what they need. If they are a Projector, Manifestor, or Reflector, or if they have an undefined Throat Center, they may need extra space to talk about it.

Family Emotional Environment

1. Who in your family has a defined ESP?
2. Which channels do they have?
    a. Tribal waves—Channels 19-49, 37-40, 59-6
    b. Individual waves—Channels 39-55, 22-12
    c. Collective waves—Channels 41-30, 36-35
3. Who in your family has an undefined ESP?
    a. How do you break auric (physical) space when the emotions become too intense?
4. How did you perceive their emotions before learning about emotions through Human Design?
5. How has your perception shifted since learning about emotions through Human Design?
6. How do you allow everyone's emotional needs to be met?

Undefined + Undefined ESP Relationships

1. How do you notice that someone has brought an emotion into the environment from an outside source? How do you let it go? How do you communicate that you need some space to let the emotions calm down before continuing?
2. How do you reset yourself when you've been around emotional people or situations?
3. What does your undefined ESP partner or child need when the emotional climate is intense? What do you need?
4. How long do you need to reset after ping-ponging emotions back and forth?
5. What do you notice about your ability to understand your emotions when you are alone or with someone who is emotionally undefined versus an emotionally defined person?

Defined + Defined ESP Relationships

1. What do you notice about your/their reaction to the emotions of others?
2. What emotional wave(s) do you both have, and do you notice the different wave types in the other person?
3. Is it easier or harder for you to experience emotional energy with another defined or undefined emotional person?
4. How do you and this other person communicate your needs in your relationship?
5. How do you honor each other's needs in your relationship?
6. How do you take responsibility for your emotional needs and expressions?

CHAPTER SIX

CENTERS

Defined centers tell us about the consistent energy we broadcast into the world, while our undefined centers show us where we're receiving the energy themes of those centers. There are two pressure centers (Head and Root), three awareness centers (Ajna, Spleen, ESP), four motor centers (Sacral, Will, ESP, Root), one manifestation center (Throat), and one identity center (G).

Conditioning in the centers is seen through energy themes. The overall theme of each center tells us about the type of energy it represents, while the gates tell us more about the specifics of each theme. If you have a channel, notice what the energy themes of the gates of that channel are. For example, Channel 19-49. Gate 19 is in the Root Center, which has a theme of pressure, while Gate 49 is in the ESP, with a theme of feeling. Begin thinking about how the theme of pressure from the Root Center affects how you experience the theme of feeling, creativity, and passion in Gate 49 when connected by a channel from how you might experience Gate 49 as a hanging gate (gate defined but not a channel). You could next look at whether anyone in your family or close friends has Gate 19 defined in their chart. Consider how you experience the energy of this channel in a relationship, and how you may experience your Gate 49 differently with others. You can do this with any of the gates/channels in your chart to gain a deeper awareness of how these energies affect you and your relationships.

As a reminder, we all have all of the chart, but how we experience it is different based on what is defined and undefined in our birth chart, as well as our conditioning. What we have defined in our chart is where we are learning about those energies through our personal experiences, whereas what is undefined in our chart is learned about through our relationships. The defined aspects of our chart are more consistent for us to work with as they are always present with us and help us understand our presence in this world. The undefined aspects help us understand other people and the pieces of ourselves that we find a little trickier at times to access and understand. We are always learning through our entire chart.

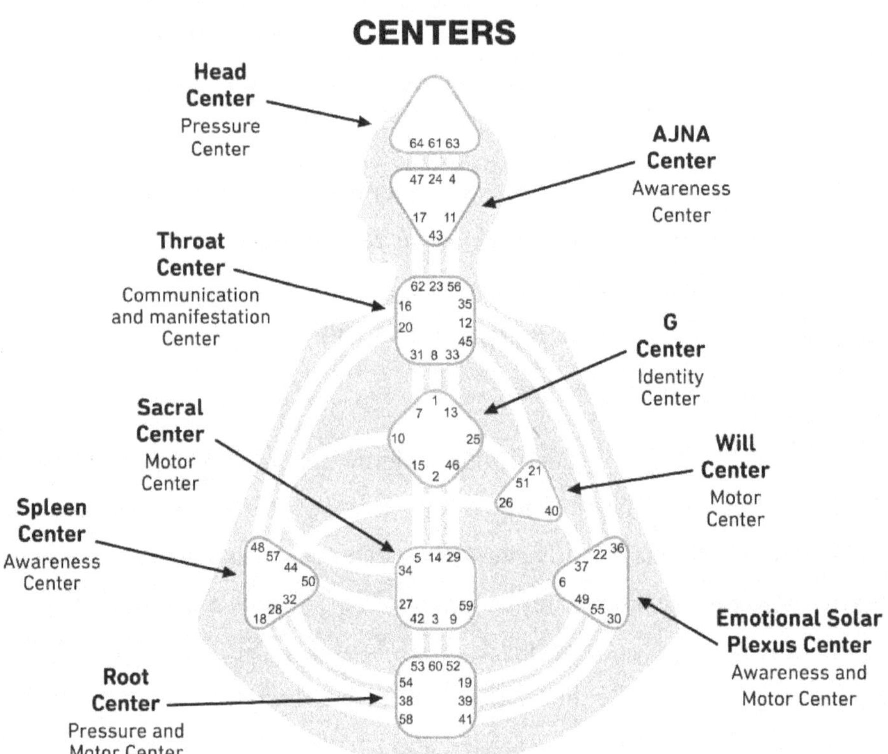

Look at the center definition that each family member has.

1. Who has the same centers defined?
2. Who has the same centers undefined? (Not colored in, but have gates activated.)
3. Who has them completely open? (No hanging gate activations anywhere in the center.)
4. Who exerts pressure (energetically) on others in your family? Anyone who has a defined Head or Root Center will create the pressure that the open Head and Root Center feel.

5. Who has motor center energy? How might that affect those without any motors (Root, ESP, Will, Sacral) or fewer motors defined?
6. Who has a defined G Center? Do you notice that they influence those without a defined G Center?
7. What do you notice about anyone in your family with an undefined Throat Center in contrast to those with a defined Throat Center (some Generators or Projectors) or a motorized Throat Center (Manifestors or Manifesting Generators)?
8. What do you notice about the sensitivity, intuition, or insight anyone with defined awareness centers (Ajna, Spleen, ESP) has, and how it affects those who do not have these centers defined?

Throughout this section, we will break down each of the centers into more specific questions to get to know them and their energy a little more. You'll notice that I share the names of the gates for each of the centers. This is meant to give you a quick keynote reference to the energy archetype of that gate.

As you go through these journal prompts, first explore your defined/undefined centers and then use the journal questions to explore the defined/undefined centers of your children, partner or parents, as you explore the parent-child relationships in your life.

Head Center Keynotes
Center for Inspiration | Pressure Center

Gates of the Head Center

64 - Before Completion - The Gate of Confusion

61 - Inner Truth - The Gate of Mystery

63 - After Completion - The Gate of Doubt

Head Center Open/Undefined ~ 70 Percent of the Population

1. Do you get lost in the pressure to have big ideas and be inspiring?
2. Do you allow yourself to daydream and not get attached to manifesting all the ideas you feel inspired by in your day?

3. Who in your family has an undefined Head Center? What do you notice about them or yourself and their or your ideas?

4. What does it mean to you to be a daydreamer? What associations do you have with the term *daydreamer*? Is it okay for you or your child to daydream? How do you not get lost in following every thought or idea? How do you help your child use their inner Authority to guide them in what inspirations to follow?

5. How can you see Head Center openness as a gift?

6. Who in your family has an **undefined** Head Center?

What do you need to learn?

- To follow your inner Authority to know which inspirations are for you versus merely interesting ideas to watch manifest around you.
- To not let the pressure to be inspiring cause you to doubt your abilities to do great things.
- To not let the pressure to know overwhelm you.

Affirmations for the Undefined Head Center

I am inspired by others and see so many possibilities! I must take notice not to try to follow all of them and know that by following my Strategy and Authority, I will know when the timing is right for me to act on inspiration.

Head Center Defined ~ 30 Percent of the Population

1. What do you notice about yourself and your ideas?

2. Do you get stuck in your way of thinking, thus limiting your view?

3. What can you do to support yourself to open your mind to other ways of thinking?

4. What other ways of communicating can help you to see another point of view?

5. Do you stop to witness the wisdom and curiosity that comes out of the people around you?

6. How can you see your Head Center definition as a gift?
7. Who in your family has a **defined** Head Center?

What do you need to learn?

- To take pauses and learn to quiet the mind.
- To use creative expression to process the inspirations your mind receives.
- To use your inner Authority to know what inspirations are for you versus what is to be shared with others. That you don't have to manifest them all.

Affirmations for the Defined Head Center

I am filled with inspiration, which I share with others through just being me. I don't have to DO anything to be inspiring. I just am when I allow myself to be me. I know that not all inspirations are for me to follow, and I use my Strategy and Authority to know which ideas are right for me while freely sharing ideas with others. I release these ideas out into the world with a blessing for whomever they are meant for when the timing is right.

Ajna Center Keynotes
Awareness Center | Process and Store Information

Gates of the Ajna Center

47 - Oppression - The Gate of Realization

24 - The Return - The Gate of Rationalization

4 - Youthful Folly - Gate of Formulization

11 - Peace - The Gate of Ideas

43 - Breakthrough - The Gate of Insight

17 - Following - The Gate of Opinion

Ajna Center Open/Undefined ~ 53 Percent of the Population

1. Are there times you can recall saying you were 100 percent certain about something, and inside, you weren't? How did that work out?
2. Do you or your child feel pressure to be certain about decisions, or do you allow yourselves to stay open to changing your minds?
3. Do you see your uncertainty as the gift it is? Or have you been conditioned to believe that you must be certain? How has that affected your life?
4. How can you see Ajna Center openness as a gift?
5. Who in your family has an **undefined** Ajna Center?

What do you need to learn?

- That you are not designed to be 100 percent certain but to remain open to all the possibilities.
- That you have an endless way of approaching ideas and processing thoughts, thus creating many new possibilities in the world.

Affirmations for the Undefined Ajna Center

I enjoy a very open mind. One where I can see things from multiple angles and don't have to get stuck in a fixed way of thinking. This allows me not to have to worry about being certain indefinitely. I do not have to hold onto certainty for the sake of being right. It is perfectly normal for me to take in new information and change my thinking. I am not wishy-washy—I am open to new ways of thinking.

Ajna Center Defined ~ 47 Percent of the Population

1. Do you recognize when you or your child are stuck in your ways of thinking?
2. How do you open your mind to other ways of thinking?
3. How does having a defined Ajna benefit you or your child? How has it limited you?
4. How can you see Ajna Center definition as a gift?
5. Who in your family has a **defined** Ajna Center?

What do you need to learn?

- To listen to other people's ideas and see another point of view.
- To know that you have a consistent way of processing information, but at times it may limit your thinking.

Affirmations for the Defined Ajna Center

Though I have a consistent way of processing information and can do so quickly, I stay open to the ideas of others. Though I can be quite certain in my thinking, as new information comes to light I remember that my way of thinking may need to change, and I remain open to hearing other ideas.

Throat Center Keynotes
Manifestation and Communication Center

Gates of the Throat Center

62 - Preponderance of the Small - The Gate of Details

23 - Splitting Apart - The Gate of Assimilation

56 - The Wanderer - The Gate of Stimulation

35 - Progress - The Gate of Change

12 - Standstill - The Gate of Caution

45 - Gathering Together - The Gate of the Gatherer

33 - Retreat - The Gate of Privacy

8 - Holding Together - The Gate of Contribution

31 - Influence - The Gate of Influence

20 - Contemplation - The Gate of the Now

16 - Enthusiasm - The Gate of Skills

Voices of the Throat Center

(AJNA) Gate 62 - I think/I don't think

(AJNA) Gate 23 - I know/I don't know

(AJNA) Gate 56 - I believe/I don't believe

(ESP) Gate 35 - I feel and usually like a change

(ESP) Gate12 - I know I can try if I'm in the mood

(ESP) Gate 45 - I have, or I don't have

(G Center) Gate 33 - I remember/I don't remember

(G Center) Gate 8 - I know I can make a contribution or not

(G Center) Gate 31 - I lead or not

(SPLEEN) Gate 20 - I am now or not

(SPLEEN) Gate 16 - I experiment or not

Throat Center Open ~ 28 Percent of the Population

1. Do you or your child struggle to be heard?
2. Did you as a child, or does your child, act out or get louder to get more attention and be heard? If so, how were you parented? And how do you handle your child when they behave this way? What meanings do you hold when a child acts silly or loud or interjects themselves in conversations that don't concern them? Knowing what you now know about the open Throat Center, would you handle this situation differently?
3. What is your or your child's biggest struggle or pain around being heard in family or friendship dynamics?
4. What does it mean to wait to share until invited or for something to respond to? How do you feel about waiting?

5. How can you see Throat Center's openness as a gift?
6. Who in your family has an **undefined** Throat Center?

What do you need to learn?

- Wait to be invited to share or to have something to respond to, so that you will be better heard.
- When you haven't been invited to the conversation and share anyway, others may subconsciously take your ideas and share them as if they were their own.

Affirmations for the Undefined Throat Center

I know that what I have to say has value; therefore, I wait for the right timing to share so that it can be received as I intend it. I do not have to compete for attention to be heard. When I am patient, I am invited to share.

Throat Center Defined ~ 72 Percent of the Population

1. Do you know how powerful your voice is?
2. What do you notice about how others respond to you or your child versus someone with an open Throat Center?
3. What is your or your child's Throat Center connected to? The centers connected to the Throat Center will tell you more about your voice.
4. How can you see Throat Center definition as a gift?
5. Who in your family has a **defined** Throat Center?

What do you need to learn?

- That your voice has an impact and can influence others.
- That you must allow others to share in the conversation.

Affirmations for the Defined Throat Center

I communicate easily and can command the attention of others. I have a responsibility not to overpower others and allow them to have their voice heard as well. I invite others to share their insights, feelings, instincts, fears, and themselves.

G Center Keynotes
Identity | Self-love | Direction

Gates of the G Center

1 - The Creative - The Gate of Self-Expression

13 - The Fellowship of Man - The Gate of the Listener

25 - Innocence - The Gate of the Spirit of the Self

46 - Pushing Upward - The Gate of the Determination of the Self

2 - The Receptive - The Gate of Direction of the Self

15 - Modesty - The Gate of Extremes

10 - Treading - The Gate of the Behavior of the Self

7 - The Army - The Role of the Self in Interaction

G Center Open ~ 43 Percent of the Population

1. Do you or your child adapt easily to new surroundings? Do you or your child listen to your body or internal cues that an environment is incorrect for you?
2. Have you or your child been accused of imitating others? If so, write about that experience.
3. If you answered yes to question two, what would you tell that younger version of yourself about that experience now that you understand the open G Center can literally take on the identity of others as part of their life experience?

4. How can you see G Center openness as a gift?
5. Who in your family has an **undefined** G Center?

What do you need to learn?

- To listen to your body when it tells you an environment is not correct for you.
- To allow yourself to experience life through other people's identities.
- To not be rigid in a fixed direction in life and to let life lead you where you need to go through your Strategy and Authority.

Affirmations for the Undefined G Center

I am here to experience many different people, places, and love. I fully embrace the chameleon-like quality I get to experience through the people I meet. I embrace others through their identity and can easily relate to them in this way. I am open to where I will go next, though it must feel right for me to enjoy it and be the correct path for me. The environment is critical to me feeling good and making aligned decisions.

G Center Defined ~ 57 Percent of the Population

1. Do you feel safe being who you truly are?
2. Do you allow yourself to show up as your authentic self?
3. Have you tried to force yourself to be someone other than who you are? If so, how did that turn out?
4. How can you see G Center definition as a gift?
5. Who in your family has a **defined** G Center?

What do you need to learn?

- To decondition from others' influence of who you should be.
- To let Strategy and Authority guide you along the trajectory of your life.
- To live out the highest expression of the gates defined in your G Center.

- To trust that you will end up just where you're supposed to be when you surrender to your Strategy and Authority to guide you.

Affirmations for the Defined G Center

I am who I am. I do not need to try to be anyone else. Everything I do is infused with the essence of me and my identity. I am consistently me, and I feel secure in my lovability. I am confident in who I am and the direction I am going in life, even if I don't know how I will get there.

Spleen Center Keynotes
Awareness Center | Fears | Intuition | Instinct

Gates of the Spleen Center

48 - The Well - The Gate of Depth

57 - The Gentle - The Gate of Intuitive Clarity

44 - Coming to Meet - The Gate of Alertness

50 - The Cauldron - The Gate of Values

32 - Duration - The Gate of Continuity

28 - Preponderance of the Great - The Gate of the Game Player

18 - Work on What Has Been Spoilt - The Gate of Correction

Affirmations of the Spleen Center

Gate 48 - The fear of inadequacy can be turned into "I can sense when I need to know more and can take action to learn what I need to know. I also know that I'll know what I need to know when I need to know it."

Gate 57 - The fear of the future can be turned into "I can sense that change is coming, and I don't need to fear it. I use my senses to take any action necessary to prepare when the time is right."

Gate 44 - The fear of the past can be turned into "I have had this experience before, I have learned from it, and I now navigate this situation with what I've learned. I can sense what I need to move forward."

Gate 50 - The fear of responsibility (for others) can be turned into "I can sense when someone is hurting and needs support, but I am not required to rescue anyone."

Gate 32 - The fear of failure can be turned into "I don't need to fear failure because when I trust in the right timing, I will know when the time is right for me to take action. Whatever happens, when I try, I learn."

Gate 28 - The fear of death can be turned into "Life is an adventure, and some adventures teach me to know what's worth standing up for. I know when to take action, when something is worth struggling for, and when to quit."

Gate 18 - The fear of authority can be turned into "I can see where patterns need correcting, but I will wait to be invited to share what I know so that it can be helpful to others."

Spleen Center Open ~ 47 Percent of the Population

1. How do you feel about your immune system?
2. Do you hold onto things or people longer than is good for you? Write about it.
3. Do you sense other people's needs, fears, or ailments? If yes, describe what that feels like, and how you separate from them?
4. How do you relate to your fears?
5. How can you see Spleen Center openness as a gift?
6. Who in your family has an **undefined** Spleen Center?

What do you need to learn?

- To let go when a relationship needs to conclude.
- To let go of things and not hold onto them out of fear or lack.
- To work on understanding self versus other and not taking on other people's fears, needs, or ailments as if they were your own.

Affirmations for the Undefined Spleen Center

My intuition speaks to me in varied ways, often depending on who I am with. I listen and share when the timing is right or have been invited. My sensitivity to the environment is one of my superpowers. It tells me when something may be a danger or threat to my health and well-being. I listen to my sensitivity to tell me when to use caution or to proceed. I do not hold onto things longer than necessary.

Spleen Center Defined ~ 53 Percent of the Population

1. Do you take care of your physical body in a preventative way? Or do you ignore it until it protests to the point that you need to pay attention to it, for example, with illness or injury?
2. Do you get stuck in the fear patterns of your defined gates, or are you consciously aware of them and use tools to manage them when they emerge?
3. Do you notice that your child or other people with an open Spleen Center tend to want to be near you or are more attached to you?
4. *This can possibly bring up some triggering memories, so please use care with yourself as you explore this territory and seek support if needed.* Do you trust your inner instinctive knowing or do you question it? Write about a time when you trusted your gut sense that something was not right or safe, and then write about a time when you did not trust your gut sense about something and realized you had a warning sign beforehand. This can be explored through small things such as not getting in your car due to a feeling you had and then finding out about an accident that occurred on that part of the road at the same time, for example.
5. How can you see Spleen Center definition as a gift?
6. Who in your family has a **defined** Spleen Center?

What do you need to learn?

- To take care of your body in a preventative way.
- To be aware of the fears associated with your defined spleen gates and use or learn tools to help manage those fears.
- To trust your knowing.

Affirmations for the Defined Spleen Center

I know things. I don't always know how I know, but I can trust that I know. I do not have to have an explanation for my knowing. I listen to what my body needs and give my body the rest and attention it needs.

Sacral Center Keynotes
Motor Center | Vitality | Life Force Energy | Workforce Energy

Gates of the Sacral Center

5 - Waiting - The Gate of Fixed Patterns

14 - Possession in Great Measure - The Gate of Power Skills

29 - The Abysmal - The Gate of Perseverance

59 - Dispersion - The Gate of Sexuality

9 - The Taming of the Power of the Small - The Gate of Focus

3 - Difficulty at the Beginning - The Gate of Ordering

42 - Increase - The Gate of Growth

27 - Nourishment - The Gate of Caring

34 - The Power of the Great - The Gate of Power

Sacral Center Open ~ 30 Percent of the Population

1. How do you notice your natural workforce energy versus what belongs to other people?
2. Do you make sure to allow yourself downtime each day?
3. Do you push yourself through *doing* to prove yourself?
4. Do you know when enough is enough?
5. How can you see Sacral Center openness as a gift?
6. Who in your family has an **undefined** Sacral Center?

What do you need to learn?

- To take downtime each day and allow the Sacral energy to discharge from your body. This can include movement.
- To learn to know when enough is enough and your energy levels are depleted.
- To consciously use the Sacral energy around you to work intentionally, but not rely on it to overwork.
- To be conscious of responding with yes/no answers as if you were a Generator type. Allow yourself to drop into your body and use your inner Authority to guide you.

Affirmations for the Undefined Sacral Center

Even though I can work at super speed at times, I know this is not sustainable for me. I am not here to DO like others. I will have plenty of energy when I enter into the correct work and agreements through my Strategy and Authority. I allow myself plenty of time to rest, reset, and discharge the energy I pick up throughout the day. Resting in bed before I fall asleep soothes my nervous system and is necessary, and I embrace this about myself.

Sacral Center Defined ~ 70 Percent of the Population

1. Do you make sure to move your body enough each day to easily and deeply sleep? If so, how? If not, what could you do to move your body more?
2. Do you allow others around you with an open Sacral Center to have downtime without pressuring them to do more?
3. Do you view other people or your child with open Sacral Centers as lazy?
4. Do you listen to your Sacral to guide you? Do you allow your child's Sacral to guide them?
5. Do you know what your Sacral feels like when it says yes or no? If so, how does it feel? If not, who can you practice asking Sacral questions with to activate this decision-making center? (Sacral Questions can be found in the appendix of *Parenting the Child You Have*, the book)
6. How can you see Sacral Center definition as a gift?
7. Who in your family has a **defined** Sacral Center?

What do you need to learn?

- To move your body enough each day.
- To activate and use your Sacral sounds to guide you.
- To care for yourself.
- To not pick up all the work that no one else wants to do, especially as parents.
- To wait for life to bring you things to respond to rather than pushing with your mind to make choices.

Affirmations for the Defined Spleen Center

I have the ability to give a lot of my energy to the things in life that I respond to. I enter into those things correctly through my Strategy and inner Authority to sustain them. I am conscious that I must care for myself first before giving to others, and I am not required to save anyone. I find the correct things to use my energy for when I wait for the right timing through Strategy and Authority. I do not have to go looking for life, as it will always come to me.

Will Center Keynotes
Willpower | Ego | Integrity | Self-Worth | Resources | Motor Center

Gates of the Will Center

21 - Biting Through - The Gate of the Hunter/Huntress

40 - Deliverance - The Gate of Aloneness

26 - The Taming Power of the Great - The Gate of the Egoist

51 - The Arousing - The Gate of Shock

Will Center Open ~ 65 Percent of the Population

1. Can you recall a time you felt disappointed that you couldn't commit to a task as you'd hoped? How did you handle it? What was your self-talk?
2. Knowing that you are not designed to have strong, lasting willpower, how would you allow yourself more grace when entering commitments?
3. Rather than committing to a task only to lose willpower, or avoiding confrontation about why the task was not met, how would you see yourself if you started saying, "I'll try" or "I'll do my best, but I can't promise I can meet that deadline."
4. How can you see Will Center openness as a gift?
5. Who in your family has an **undefined** Will Center?

What do you need to learn?

- That it's okay to say "I'll try" rather than "I promise."
- That you are not designed to hold willpower constantly long-term.
- Your self-worth does not come from what/how much you do.
- That you are worthy just because you exist.

Affirmations for the Undefined Will Center

I am careful not to enter into agreements on a whim without relying on my Strategy and checking in with my Authority. I am aware that I can easily overcommit if I am not listening to my Authority. I allow myself the grace to respectfully decline or let others know that I will try but cannot promise the outcome they desire. I do not prove my worth through my doing. I know my value. I am inherently worthy.

Will Center Defined ~ 35 Percent of the Population

1. How do you feel knowing that 65 percent of people do not have consistent willpower?
2. How can you offer more grace to others when asking for commitments from them?
3. How do you allow yourself cycles of rest between pushes of willpower?
4. How can you see Will Center definition as a gift?
5. Who in your family has a **defined** Will Center?

What do you need to learn?

- To allow cycles of rest.
- To give others grace who have open Will Centers.
- Your word holds a promise and you should only commit to things you are truly ready to commit to. Notify those who will be impacted if you cannot meet the commitment.

Affirmations for the Defined Will Center

Though I can make a commitment and stick with it, I also know I cannot rely on willpower continuously and need cycles of rest. When I rest, I come back and support myself and others in a more resourced way. I give grace to others who do not have the same level of willpower that I do, and I understand their ability to remain committed may wane.

Emotional Solar Plexus (ESP) Center Keynotes
Awareness Center | Feelings | Moods | Creativity | Passion | Desire

Gates of the ESP Center

36 - The Darkening of the Light - The Gate of Crisis

22 - Grace - The Gate of Openness

37 - The Family - The Gate of Friendship

6 - Conflict - The Gate of Friction

49 - Revolution - The Gate of Principles

55 - Abundance - The Gate of Spirit

30 - The Clinging Fire - The Gate of Feelings

ESP Center Open ~ 49 Percent of the Population

1. How do you identify emotions that come from you versus those you feel from others?
2. Do you avoid conflict or confrontation due to how it feels? If so, describe what conflict or confrontation feels like in your body. What are some ways or tools you have that you can use to manage the intensity of those feelings? Do you use them? Where do you think you could find the tools if you don't feel like you

currently have the tools to manage this? What modalities or support sound interesting to learn more about?

3. Is there anyone in your home with a defined ESP that you have difficulty communicating with because of the emotional intensity? If so, whom? And how does this show up in your relationship? How would you like the relationship to shift?
4. What are some ways to allow others' emotions to move through you?
5. Can you allow yourself to sit with other people's uncomfortable emotions without offering to fix the problem or give more than you have to give?
6. How do you give yourself space to discharge the emotions you pick up from others in your day-to-day life? Your child? Your partner? People at work?
7. How can you see ESP Center openness as a gift?
8. Who in your family has an **undefined** ESP Center?

What do you need to learn?

- Boundaries around what is emotionally yours versus someone else's.
- To learn techniques that help manage stress.
- That your emotional empathy can become your greatest gift.
- To let emotions move through you and not let them get stuck in you.
- That what you feel from others is not a reflection of you. You don't have to assume that you did something wrong.

Affirmations for the Undefined ESP Center

I recognize that the emotions I feel around others are meant for me to experience but not to hold onto. They are not mine; I am simply a witness to them. I connect with others and understand their emotional state and needs, but I do not have to take responsibility for them. I trust what I feel. I know how to take care of myself when the emotional environment has been intense or continuous. I allow myself plenty of time to reset and release others' emotions.

ESP Center Defined ~ 51 Percent of the Population

1. Do you know what wave(s) you have? What are they? How do they operate?
2. What do you notice about your wave(s)? Are your highs and lows extreme? Do you feel like you spend more time in the highs or the lows, or somewhere in between?
3. How many other people with emotional waves are in your home? What are the different wave types? (See chapter five on emotions for wave types).
4. How many emotionally undefined people are in your home? How do they react to your highs and lows?
5. Is there anything you'd like to be different about how you experience your wave and how it affects your child or others in your life?
6. How can you see ESP Center definition as a gift?
7. Who in your family has a **defined** ESP Center?

What do you need to learn?

- What emotional wave(s) you have and how they operate.
- To take care of your emotional needs. I.e., time alone, support, hugs, verbal processing, etc.
- That your emotional wave is constantly projecting out to others and that it affects them, especially children.
- Understand what each of the waves need and learn how to ask for those needs to be met *before* they become an issue.

Affirmations for the Defined ESP Center

I do not jump into decisions because I honor my decision-making process. I allow myself the time I need and do not let pressure overwhelm me. If the opportunity disappears before I have reached clarity, I know it was not for me at this time. There are more opportunities available to me that are correct for me. I am aware of my emotional wave(s) and help the people in my life understand them so that I can allow them to flow more gently through me. I do not get stuck identifying with my wave because I am so much more than a single emotion.

Root Center Keynotes
Pressure Center | Motor Center

Gates of the Root Center

58 - The Joyous - The Gate of Vitality

38 - Opposition - The Gate of the Fighter

54 - The Marrying Maiden - The Gate of Drive

53 - Development - The Gate of Beginnings

60 - Limitation - The Gate of Acceptance

52 - Keeping Still (Mountain) - The Gate of Stillness

19 - Approach - The Gate of Wanting

39 - Obstruction - The Gate of Provocation

41 - Decrease - The Gate of Contraction

Root Center Open ~ 40 Percent of the Population

1. What can you do to get more comfortable sitting with the idea that there will always be pressure in your life that you will want to be free from?

2. What techniques do you have experience with to calm your nervous system? I.e., deep breathing, meditation, yoga, drawing, creating, EFT, etc.
3. What effect has external pressure had on you growing up and as an adult? Did your parents or family members in your home have a defined Root Center? Do you have a child or partner with a defined Root Center in your home now?
4. If your child has a defined Root Center, how does that pressure show up in your parenting?
5. Can you feel the adrenaline in your body from the pressure of other people? What does it feel like? How do you recognize it? What do you do with it?
6. How do you release pressure from your body?
7. How can you see Root Center openness as a gift?
8. Who in your family has an **undefined** Root Center?

What do you need to learn?

- To find ways to be comfortable or at least aware of the pressure from others and use it consciously.
- To find ways to discharge the adrenalized pressure energy you pick up from others throughout the day.
- To take a pause when someone's request feels like they want it done now, and ask yourself if that is true or if it just feels that way.

Affirmations for the Undefined Root Center

I understand that no matter how much I do, I will always feel a certain amount of pressure to do more. I am not here to push or continuously allow myself to run on adrenaline, and I take time to rest. When I feel pressure from others, I pause and consider if I truly need to act in the moment or if I am simply amplifying the pressure to DO from others. I allow plenty of time to slow down and enjoy life, even when I feel pressure. I sit with pressure as a normal feeling and use it consciously.

Root Center Defined ~ 60 Percent of the Population

1. What is your relationship with time and timing? Are you someone who is on time or running on your own schedule? How has that affected your life?
2. Do you have a child or partner with an open Root Center? How do you notice they respond to your requests? Does it feel like pressure to them? What would they say about how they feel pressure from you? This relationship dynamic has the potential to feel like there is a lot of pressure behind your requests, but this does not mean that you're pressuring them as they may feel you are, and can create a lot of misunderstandings.
3. What center does your Root Center connect to? Those channels tell you more about how you feel pressure. Root Center to Spleen Center is the pressure to keep yourself, kids, and family safe and healthy and can also manifest as fears of the future, past, authority, taking action, failing, or being wrong about something. Root Center to Sacral Center is the pressure to work and do. Root Center to ESP is the pressure to feel and create experiences that make you feel deeply. How do you experience these channels?
4. How do you allow yourself to pull back and pause when the energy to push and do is not there? When you're working hard on a project, and it feels like you're not getting anywhere, do you allow yourself to rest and pause until the pulse returns?
5. How can you see Root Center definition as a gift?
6. Who in your family has a **defined** Root Center?

What do you need to learn?

- To recognize that you will have periods of pressure to do and periods where you won't feel the pressure to do. This is a normal cycle.
- How you experience the pressure coming from the Root Center.
- How others feel pressure from you and understand how this energetic dynamic can help you see where conflict might arise.

Affirmations for the Defined Root Center

I feel the drive to do things in my own timing, and I honor the cycles of rest that I need to have the energy required for the task. I do not push against right timing and listen to what my body needs. When I listen and the Root Center pulse switches on, I can get much done in a short amount of time. When I keep pushing while the pulse is off, I spend a lot of time getting a little done; therefore, I listen to this pulse and use my energy wisely.

CHAPTER SEVEN

PROFILE LINES

The Profile lines tell more about your tendencies and needs as you interact with the world. The first number in your Profile comes from the Conscious Sun, and the second number comes from the Unconscious Sun. I find that the younger someone is, the more they tend to identify with the characteristics of their Conscious Sun Profile line and tend not to be able to see the Unconscious Sun Profile line until they've lived more life and have more to reflect upon. They may also begin to see it more after becoming aware of it through their Human Design.

The Profile lines 1 through 6 are listed here. Please make sure to look up both of your Profile lines in *Parenting the Child You Have*, the book, to see how they complement or contradict one another. For example, the 1/3 Profile is someone who, through their 1st line Profile, needs to have enough information to feel comfortable moving forward and sharing what they know, while the 3rd line needs to experiment and try things to see how it works for them. This can leave someone with this Profile feeling either like they don't know enough and are afraid to try for they might fail, or they may jump into everything without doing enough research and feel like they can't ever do anything right as it takes more trial and error to figure out what works. These two Profile lines complement each other because when you have a bit of information, it makes it easier to make an educated guess on what would work best, and then you can be more successful with fewer repeating steps through your 3rd line process.

Please reference *Parenting the Child You Have*, the book, for more details on the Profile lines' qualities.

Line 1

NEED - To have enough knowledge to feel secure.

DRIVE - To ensure the safety of all.

FEAR - That they don't know enough, which can keep them stuck from moving forward.

DESIRE - To be a fountain of knowledge for self and others.

For 1st Line Parents

1. What are some areas as parents where you are always researching how to parent your child?
   a. Do you let a lack of *enough* knowledge stop you from taking action?
2. What does it mean to you to know *enough*?
3. How do you allow your children or family to learn in their own way?
4. Do you trust the knowing of others who cannot back up their knowing with citations?
5. What would it take for you to lean into other ways of knowing?
6. How do you perceive yourself when you don't know the answer to something? Is it okay for you not to know all the answers? What does it mean to you if you don't know the answer?

For Parents of 1st Line Children

1. How do you encourage your child to learn?
2. Does your child have access to reliable sources of information?
3. How do you teach them what a reliable or credible source of information is?
4. Do you ever push your child to share what they know before they're ready?
5. How do you honor them when they say they're not ready to share yet, but also not allow them to hide away in their learning and never share what they know?

Line 2

NEED - Time alone to retreat and integrate what they know.

DRIVE - Explore and learn in their own way on their own time.

FEAR - They will be called out before they're ready and/or everyone will forget about them.

DESIRE - To be allowed time to explore their passions and left alone until ready to emerge.

For 2nd Line Parents

1. How do you allow yourself to retreat and have time alone? If you don't, what are some ways you could carve out a bit of time for you to get the solitude you crave?
2. Do you trust your innate knowing?
3. How do you react when people call you out to share your knowledge?
4. Do you fear that you might disappear and no one would notice, or you'd be forgotten?
5. What do you do when you have time alone?
6. Do you allow yourself to be nourished by solitude, or do you try to fill it with busy work?

For Parents of 2nd Line Children

1. What do you notice about your child's need to have quiet time to themselves?
2. Do you allow them quiet time or try to pull them out to be more social?
3. What feelings or thoughts do you have about a child spending time alone?
4. Is your child quiet and introspective? If so, what thoughts, feelings, or worries do you have about that side of them?

Line 3

NEED - To explore and learn through doing.

DRIVE - To see how things work and why or why not.

FEAR - That they will fail.

DESIRE - To be allowed the space to explore and experiment without feeling judged for the outcome.

For 3rd Line Parents

1. Do you embrace this learn-by-doing aspect of your design?
2. What ideas do you hold about trying something and not having it work out immediately?
3. What does failure mean to you? What beliefs do you hold about failing?
4. How did your parents/family react to your way of learning by doing?
5. What are/were your parents' Profiles (if you have this info)? How did their Profiles influence the expression of your 3rd line energy?

For Parents of 3rd Line Children

1. Do you allow your child to try things without being certain that they will work out as planned?
2. What does it feel like to let your child learn through doing when you can clearly see that it won't work out as they'd hoped? Do you let them do it anyway (as long as it's not harmful)?
3. How can you reframe the idea that you are failing to support your child in their learning process?
4. How does your child's "let's try it and see" attitude affect you?

Line 4

NEED - To know what's coming next before moving forward.

DRIVE - To feel secure in their knowing and have a solid foundation and network to count on.

FEAR - That they won't be prepared or have enough.

DESIRE - To feel secure and have enough resources and connections to fulfill their life purpose.

For 4th Line Parents

1. How adept are you at navigating change?
2. Do you make and adapt to changes easily, or do you need to know all the details before taking a leap?
3. What would happen or how would you feel if you didn't know ahead of time how things would likely work out?
4. How did you feel as a child navigating change? Were you prepared with enough information, or was there something your family could have done for you to make change easier?

For Parents of 4th Line Children

1. Do you inform your 4th line child of what to expect when taking them to new places or doing new things? If so, how? If not, how could you help them feel more secure in knowing what to expect?
2. What types of information does your child need to be able to make changes more easily?
3. What areas of life do you find are most challenging for your child to navigate change? What are some ways you could support them, knowing now that they may need more information?
4. How do you feel about having to slow down to tell your child the details of what to expect? Remember, there is no judgment here, just curiosity about what is true. Once you identify how they feel about a situation, you can begin to navigate it better and prepare them with what they need to know.

Line 5

NEED - To be seen for who they truly are.

DRIVE - To help others and share what they know.

FEAR - That they will be judged for what they are not doing or who they aren't (others' projections).

DESIRE - To be projected onto for the right reasons and to be called out to help, share what they know, and be recognized for it.

For 5th Line Parents

1. Where have others in your life placed projections onto you that were not true? How did that make you feel?
2. Where have others in your life placed projections onto you that were positive, and you felt recognized for your abilities? How did that make you feel?
3. Do you hide and not allow yourself to take up your right space in the world for fear of others' projections onto you? If so, how? And how would you like that to be different? What do you need to heal or release in order to be able to fully show up in the world as your authentic self?
4. Do you notice when you are projecting onto your child or family your expectations or ideas?
5. Have you noticed that people are just drawn to you? And do you accept or shy away from that attention?
6. Do you feel comfortable leading others? Why or why not?
7. Do others come to you for support or guidance because of your lived experience? How does it feel to share this knowledge or support?

For Parents of 5th Line Children

1. Do you find yourself arguing with your child over things that they deny or seem confused by? Is it possible that you are unintentionally projecting your wounds onto them?
2. Is your child projecting onto you, leaving you feeling confused or misunderstood?
3. Given that the 5th line also needs time alone, similar to the 2nd line, how do you honor that in your child?
4. Do you find your child stepping in to try and "save the day" often when they haven't been asked or invited? Do you allow them to always jump in, or do you try to help them navigate which things to respond to through their inner Authority?
5. Does your child see the best in you and other people? If so, what do you notice about that quality in them? Has this quality caused them pain expecting more from others than they can give or live up to?

Line 6

NEED - To be allowed to explore in their first phase of life (until their first Saturn return around age thirty), to retreat and slow down to integrate their learning in their second phase, also referred to as being "on the roof" (Saturn return until Chiron Return, around age fifty), and then to live an aligned life with the truth of who they BE, showing others how to be themselves.

DRIVE - To find and fulfill their life purpose.

FEAR - That they won't fulfill their life's mission or purpose.

DESIRE - To fulfill their life purpose and leave an impression on humanity with how they lived their life.

For 6th Line Parents

1. Did you embrace the 3rd line nature of your early life (up to your first Saturn return at approximately twenty-eight to thirty)?
2. If you are past your first Saturn return and in the "on the roof" phase, are you allowing yourself to slow down and integrate the wisdom you gained during the first phase of your 6th line life? Are you judging yourself for not being as experimental and willing to dive into everything, or are you enjoying the slower pace?
3. If you are in the third phase of your 6th line life, are you walking your talk? If not, do your children call you on it? Are you living true to the lessons you teach your children? If not, what do you need to do to bring yourself into better alignment?
4. How much emphasis do you put on DOing versus BEing?

For Parents of 6th Line Children

The childrearing years will be raising the equivalent of a 3rd line child here, so their questions will be more in line with a 3rd line Profile child.

1. Do you allow your child to try things without being certain they will work out as planned?
2. What does it feel like to let your child learn through doing when you can clearly see that it won't work out as they'd hoped? Do you let them do it anyway (as long as it's not harmful)?
3. How can you reframe the idea that you are failing to support your child in their learning process?
4. How does your child's "let's try it and see" attitude affect you?

CHAPTER EIGHT

SINGLE DEFINITION VS. SPLIT DEFINITION

Do you have a single definition, split, triple split, or quadruple split in your energy centers in your chart? Reference chapter ten in *Parenting the Child You Have*, the book, for more details on split definition.

If Someone in Your Family Has a Single-definition Chart

Who has a single definition in your family? It's important to remember that though they may want people in their life, they don't energetically need anyone else to feel complete and often feel better doing things on their own and acting more independently.

If You Have a Single-definition Chart

1. How do you notice the needs of others around you?
2. Where might you be frustrated, bitter, or angry that others "need" you more than you need them?
3. What might you need to communicate with others to let them know that your independence is not a personal avoidance of them?
4. Would sharing this aspect of your energetic self with others help to create more peace, success, or satisfaction in your relationship?

Split Charts

Having a split definition in your chart just means that it's easier for certain aspects of yourself to be expressed around other people or through certain transits in the Human

Design system of the planets passing through and temporarily defining the gates throughout the year.

1. Who has a split definition in your family? What gates or channels bridge the split?
2. Who has a triple split in your family? What gates or channels bridge the splits?
3. Who has a quadruple split in your family? What gates or channels bridge the splits?
4. If you have splits, triple, or quad splits in your family, does anyone else in the family have the gates or channels defined that bridge those splits? If so, who? Make note of what definition each person has, to better understand who they may connect best with. They may find it easier to talk, emote, do, sense, or think with some people over others.

If You Have a Split Chart Definition

1. What do you notice about your relationships with people who have a single-definition chart?
2. Do you feel you need them more than they need you?
3. What would it take to release the desire to feel needed in return?
4. How might you be judging yourself for needing others?
5. How can you find understanding and peace in knowing that you *energetically* need others while someone important to you does not?

CHAPTER NINE

REFLECTING ON THE JOURNEY

As we come to the end of our journey together in this workbook, I invite you to go back to the beginning and review your initial thoughts on your childhood, your parenting, and your children when you began and write about how you see things now.

1. What has shifted?
2. Who do you see differently? How?
3. Is there anyone in your life you'd like to talk to about your new awareness?
4. How do you see yourself? Your parents/caregivers? Your child(ren)?
5. How can you stay connected to the truth of who you are? What do you need?
6. Have you identified what your physical or spiritual needs are? Is there anyone you need to share them with?
7. Is there anything you need to do to release the past and allow space for something new to grow? If so, what? When will you do it?

Remember to go back to the five-step process in chapter two for any areas you feel stuck around or find challenging to help shift and let go of conditioning or patterns that are holding you back.

As you continue to explore and evolve, you may come back and complete these exercises and contemplations again and again. Families change, people change, and circumstances definitely change. Thoughts that once served us can become limiting and unhelpful. Human Design can help guide you back to your truth and a deeper understanding of the people in your life. The more life you live, the more you deepen your understanding of self and others, and repeating these exercises and journal prompts can help you integrate your new awarenesses along your journey in this life.

RESOURCES

For bonuses and to access more resources directly from Aypril Porter that accompany the book and enrich your learning experience:

- Images from *Parenting the Child You Have Workbook* in color and enlargeable
- Parenting by Human Design Classes
- Guided meditation from Chapter Two—Getting connected to your inner child
- EFT (tapping) how-to video
- Aypril's Human Design chart

Just open up the camera app, and your phone will automatically open a web browser and take you to the embedded link.

ABOUT THE AUTHOR

Aypril Porter is a Human Design 5/2 Projector. Born and raised in the Pacific Northwest to Projector and Manifesting Generator parents, she lives with her Projector daughters, Manifestor husband, and Projector mom. She has spent her entire adult life working in service to others as a Medical Assistant, Nutritional Therapy Practitioner, stay-at-home mom, and even a scuba instructor, among other jobs. She currently serves others through her Life and Human Design Coaching practice, where she helps people live the life their soul desires and bounce back from burnout. She also helps parents to raise their children in a way that allows them to remain true to themselves, so they don't have to group and have a crisis to remember the truth of who they are.

Aypril believes that we can create a world where people feel seen, heard, loved, and valued for being themselves–one where we can embrace who we authentically are and allow others to do the same. She believes that when we feel seen for who we are, we have more compassion for each other and understanding for the people who challenge us most. She is passionate about giving people the tools to develop a new life story that empowers them to live their truth and raise their children to do the same. Having personally shifted relationships with family members who always felt difficult to her by seeing them through the lens of Human Design, she is a huge advocate of the freedom found within this system. She believes that anyone can change ancestral patterns by utilizing Human Design to see beyond the emotional responses to the truth of who they and their loved ones are. She also believes people can stop the wounds of childhood from being passed onto future generations by showing up and doing the work of staying curious about what is possible.

Aypril enjoys working with clients of all ages. She is available for Human Design Sessions, Human Design Parent Coaching, Human Design Life Coaching, and classes. You can find her at www.ayprilporter.com.

For more great books from Human Design Press

Visit Books.GracePointPublishing.com

If you enjoyed reading *Parenting the Child You Have Workbook,* and purchased it through an online retailer, please return to the site and write a review to help others find the book.

www.ingramcontent.com/pod-product-compliance
Lightning Source LLC
LaVergne TN
LVHW081318110826
845149LV00006B/1543

9781961347137